To Mum,

Happy Birthday

love

Sharon, Dave
& Darrell x
March 1996.

Mothers & Daughters

Mothers & Daughters

ALISON GRAY

DEDICATION

For my mother, Mary Norris
I am glad that we had the time to become friends.

First published in 1993 by Bridget Williams Books Limited,
PO Box 11-294, Wellington, New Zealand
Reprinted 1993

ISBN 0 908912 37 4

Design by Mission Hall Design Group
Typeset by Archetype, Wellington
Printed by South Wind Production Singapore Pte Ltd

Contents

Contents

Acknowledgements

This book owes its existence to the 26 women who agreed to tell me their stories. Although they were often diffident, they were uniformly warm and welcoming. I enjoyed the company of each one of them and thank them for their hospitality as well as for the considerable effort they put into making sure their tales were well told.

Obtaining the stories was a time-consuming task. Few mothers and daughters lived in the same city and as I zig-zagged across the country I was exremely grateful for the assistance of the Women's Suffrage Centennial Trust and the New Zealand Oral History Archive. Their support enabled me to travel, buy tapes and equipment, make toll calls and have the tapes professionally transcribed. Without their help I would probably still be writing this book.

Brenda Watson did transcriptions quickly and efficiently. I appreciated her help and enjoyed working with her.

On a personal level, I am grateful as ever, to friends and family who were prepared to listen and exchange ideas, who encouraged me through the soggy bits and who cheered me on when it was going well – Garth Baker, Bronwen Webb, Jenny Neale, Alison Parr, Jane Tolerton, Jane Westaway, Vicky Wilde and Karen Ward spring immediately to mind. But all of you who have drunk coffee, eaten lunch and gone for long walks have played a part. So have the letter-writers and phone-natterers. Thank you.

Finally, thank you to Jane Parkin and Bridget Williams, who have been as professional, supportive and encouraging as always.

My Mother & Me

My mother will be 82 next month. If her body were in charge, she wouldn't be here at all. She has emphysema, diabetes and glaucoma. She has had a moderate heart attack and a mild stroke, and the ulcers on her legs take months to heal. But her body doesn't rule her life, her spirit does, and that is why she still lives alone in her small house, doing her own cooking, cleaning and ironing. She irons everything, even the wrinkle-free polyester cotton sheets. Until her heart attack, she drove herself to the doctor, the hairdresser and the shops. Now the shopping is a chore we share, touring the aisles with our respective trolleys. Mum picks over the fruit and vegetables and jokes with the clerk who weighs her apples while she leans on her trolley to catch her breath. She's a small, frail, brave figure, much shorter than me now and I wonder when that happened. There's no flesh on her bones and her fine, white hair haloes her head, contrasting sharply with the emerald-green track suits and rich pink shirts she wears in defiance of convention. Every week she buys treats to leaven her restricted diet – fillet steak, freshly cooked chicken, sockeye salmon and ham. Good on her, I think, as I plough on behind, filling my trolley with a more mundane collection. She's only been able to afford to do that in the last few years – and it's only in the last few years that we've become friends.

I was the third of six children, the second of five daughters and the third child in less than three years – all of which shaped my life. It wasn't until I was an adult that I read about the typical middle child – by that time, I could have written the book. I was attention-seeking, rebellious, unco-operative, questioning and recalcitrant. Until I had children of my own I was insensitive to Mum's exhaustion and to the struggle she had to make ends meet. If I wanted something I wanted it, often quite noisily, and flounced when I couldn't have it. I was not, in retrospect, a generous child. Underneath the truculence, I often knew that I was being unreasonable, but I persevered. I wanted to be noticed but, above all, I wanted to feel appreciated and loved and I didn't know any other way to go about it.

For most of my childhood and adolescence, we lived in an old two-storey house in Thorndon, right under Tinakori Hill. It was a plain building, with double-hung windows, peeling paint and a rickety front verandah that later subsided. My sisters and I always shared bedrooms, my brother had one to himself – an early source of rancour, but then we girls always did think he was the favourite. Looking back, I see Mum's presence in every room, above all in the kitchen, which was a vast, inconvenient space, lined with tongue-and-groove boards painted mid-green. A safe in one corner kept the butter and meat cold. Next to it was a chipheater where we burnt rubbish and other unmentionable things wrapped in newspaper. Mum cooked on an old electric stove with a rounded rim; beside it was a kauri bench which we scrubbed reluctantly every day. For most of my time at home, Mum did all the cooking, producing plain meals and sublime baking; we children did the dishes on a roster over which we fought regularly. It was in the kitchen that she dished out pocket money and money for school trips and Sunday school, and nagged us to get our school lunches cut.

Her bedroom was also her sewing room. She was often there when I came home from school, hunched over her old Robinson machine, sewing endless streams of shorts, shirts, dresses and coats. Or she might be in the dining room, sitting at the kitchen end of the vast grey formica table she and Dad had specially made to accommodate us all. She did her mending and knitting there. She also made lists, paid bills, worked out budgets and wrote excuse notes for absences from school. In the mornings the washhouse had priority, as she thrust big loads of dripping sheets and towels through the wringer in time to catch the morning breeze. She was always working, often distracted and always tired.

She was much more of a force in my life than Dad, who disappeared behind his paper every night, his toes poking out of his slippers and his cigarette ash falling on the floor when he missed the coal scuttle. He emerged only to receive cups of tea, to listen to the nine o'clock news, to reinforce instructions to go to bed or to respond absent-mindedly to questions. It was Mum who dealt with the daily issues – signing forms, sorting out squabbles, supervising chores and agreeing or not agreeing to requests. Dad came in as back-up on occasion, but we all knew it was really Mum who was in charge. Or was she? She certainly made sure we stuck to the rules, but who made the rules? I still don't know the answer to that. I just know there were lots of them, spoken and unspoken – some for us and some for Mum and Dad. Rules like: work hard, tell the truth, keep busy, do well at school, respect authority, don't take risks, don't draw attention to yourself, don't show your feelings; in fact, don't be excessive in any way in thought, word, deed or dress.

They were rules to protect and instruct but they also confined and constrained. 'Don't show your feelings' was particularly hard, because it meant that we couldn't be exuberant or passionate or excited. Above all, it meant we couldn't be angry. Any sign of conflict was instantly suppressed and one of the most heinous crimes we could commit was to answer back. It was enough to make Dad leap from his chair, glaring and shaking his newspaper at us, crying, 'Don't speak to your mother like that.' We froze in mid-speech and sulked or muttered, biting our lips. This rule kept Mum's authority intact and the house quiet, but it was immensely frustrating and often painful. I still feel anxious when I hear raised voices or arguments of any kind and I go out of my way to placate and appease. It took me years to learn to negotiate and be flexible. I still don't do it well.

The rules for Mum and Dad were pretty simple. Dad told me about them two weeks before he died, proud that they had never been broken. They were: never praise the children in case they get swollen heads, and treat all the children the same. Never mind if they are different. He drifted off into semi-consciousness and died without knowing that he'd finally made sense of my struggles and freed me to become friends with Mum.

We didn't hug much in our family and we didn't shout, but there was still plenty of feeling between Mum and me. I remember when I was about six, I learned to knit. My first effort was disastrous and I ended up with an enormous tangle of wool that got tighter and tighter the more I tried to unravel it. I put it aside and cried. Mum was unrelenting: 'You're not getting any more wool until you untangle it.' I tried again, it got worse, I cried some more, but all to no avail. She insisted and I had to persevere for a couple more days. I learned that I should finish whatever I began, even when doing so was pointless. I've only recently been brave enough to cut my losses and move on. And I've only recently realised that Mum might have been as worried about the wool as about me – it was probably too valuable to be wasted by a six-year-old.

Mum performed miracles with money. We all went to Brownies and Guides. We went on school trips, but not holidays, and for a while the three eldest of us went to private schools. Such was the value Mum and Dad put on education and gentility. The house was full of books and we were all offered ballet and music. My ballet career was short-lived, stretching to one semi-public performance in the Irish Washerwoman's Dance at the age of about seven. I still remember Mum making the costumes and worrying about the cost of the material. I moved on to piano lessons. Mum wanted us all to learn classical piano and the others did that. I had been seduced by jazz and demanded to learn 'modern'. 'Learn classical first, then you can learn modern,' said Mum. I refused and learned nothing, and now I regret it. And I wish we had talked about it more – that might have been worth more than the piano lessons in the long run.

While I often felt hard done by, there were lots of warm, safe feelings too. Mum was there through some nasty illnesses – an infected leg, whooping cough, mumps, measles and chicken pox. She did a nice line in scrambled eggs on toast and that's still my favourite dish when I take to my bed. As I grew older I almost liked being sick. It meant I got Mum to myself for the day, the house was quiet, the days long and still, and there was time to read. Mum would always come upstairs before she went to the shops to ask if there was anything special I wanted for lunch. I usually asked for a hot pie. She wasn't one for sitting on beds and nattering – she was far too busy and ill at ease with sickness for that – but she was always, unfailingly, there.

Perhaps it was inevitable that the distance between us would increase as I moved into and through my teenage years. I can imagine Mum looking wearily across the widening gulf, wondering why it had to be so difficult and where it would end. We argued about everything – what I wore, the subjects I took at school (I wanted to take art but Mum and Dad insisted on French), when I went out, when I came home, who I went with, the music I listened to, the art I liked, how I spent my time (not enough with the family and too much in my room, not enough on homework and chores and too much in coffee bars, at the pool or on the phone), my language (too uppity or too crass), and my attitude (too insolent). I could go on, but there's not much pleasure in it and it's not very original. In fact, as I read the list now, I am surprised how absolutely normal it looks. Disagreements in the teenage years are irritating, unpleasant, exhausting, even boring, but they are normal.

Why then were those years so painful and destructive for both of us? I think it was partly to do with our family 'rules'. Not the ones about being home by 10 or catching the last bus or not going out during the week – Mum was always reasonable about matters like that and guilt at breaking those rules was always justified – but the unspoken ones about how we as a family behaved, what we liked and didn't like, even what we thought. The only way to find out about those rules was to break them. I learned somewhat painfully and sadly that we didn't go down town on Friday nights just to be one of the crowd, we didn't clamour for the latest in bobby socks as illustrated in *Seventeen* magazine, and we weren't pretentious in our tastes, drinking black coffee, watching foreign films and listening to jazz.

We had a cautious, conservative approach, just like *Scuffy the Tugboat*, one of the Little Golden Books that we read as small children. Scuffy usually lived in the bath, but one day the little boy who owned him and his father (girls didn't have tugboats in those days) took Scuffy down to the brook to play. And Scuffy floated away, off down the brook to a stream, on to a river and out towards the sea. Just before he was swept into the ocean, the little boy and his father scooped him up and returned him to the safety and security of the bathtub, and Scuffy was happy. Safe and familiar is best: that was the message. Don't take risks and don't go beyond what is proper and appropriate.

But I wanted to explore that ocean. I was obsessed with it. I even went through a period of gazing over Wellington Harbour and Cook Strait, dreaming of adventures and writing appallingly sentimental poems about the boundless, restless sea. I knew there were worlds beyond Wellington and families with other rules. So I fought hard for what I wanted, and usually won. It was a pretty uneven match. I was determined and Mum was tired. But the victories were hollow. I'd come downstairs in my latest creation to a frosty glare, and leave the house feeling miserable. I had good times, in the lonely, uncertain way that is typical of teenage exploration, never being quite sure if I was in with the in-crowd or not, but defiantly determined to carry on. I usually returned home to silence, pursed lips and a frown. I felt criticised and judged. There was no pleasure in what I'd done or seen, no excitement about films, music or art. Only puzzled feelings of shame, guilt and loneliness. My defiance increased along with the distance between us.

And that growing distance increased Mum's fear that I was up to no good. In fact, I was too timid to engage in anything very dangerous – sex was too scary, we couldn't afford alcohol, and very few people had access to cars. We walked on beaches, sat round talking or listening to music and dancing, went to the movies, drank coffee and paraded at the local swimming pool. Although we occasionally kissed hotly in the backs of cars, we were remarkably innocent. Yet I felt increasingly dirty, ashamed, angry and confused. I did very well at school, but it wasn't enough to compensate for challenging the rules. We were expected to do well, there were no Brownie points and no praise for doing what you were supposed to do, so that didn't help.

With Dad's help, I got a job in the government – it was seen as a secure option, with a sound future – and went to university part-time. I stayed at home. We lived near the university so Mum and Dad's argument that flatting was financially foolish and quite unnecessary persuaded me to stay. Unhappy as I was, I didn't want to make a final break. On the contrary, I clung to the notion that doing well at work and at university must earn at least a warm word of approval. It didn't, and I spent more and more time away from home with the boyfriend I'd met at the pool at 14 and met again when I left school at 16.

We married soon after I turned 20. He was 21. Mum and Dad disapproved strongly. We insisted, two insecure people thinking we were in love, afraid to break up in case we didn't find anyone else. And it was the only way I could see to leave home. The marriage lasted 11 years, during which time (still looking for Brownie points) I did more degrees and had three children. The children helped bridge the gap between my parents and me – they were definitely appropriate and proper – but by then we were living in another city, so there was little opportunity for closeness.

I came back to Wellington alone when the children were small. By this time Mum and Dad had retired to a small cottage on the main road in Plimmerton so that Dad could look out over the sea. His health had deteriorated so Mum spent a lot of her time caring for him. At a time when she might have looked forward to fun and freedom, she was once again constrained. With three pre-schoolers, I had a new empathy for the 30 years she had spent raising us. My heart went out to her as I felt her energy drained by the demands of Dad's illness. She liked golf, but had little time to play it; she discovered women friends at bowls, the local library and the Country Women's Institute, but had little time to spend with them. She was constantly worried and on edge as she dealt with doctors and hospitals and district nurses. I felt ashamed of how I'd behaved as a teenager and how far I had pushed her to let me do what I wanted.

Thanks to her belief in the importance of education, I had more options than she did. I had good qualifications, I liked learning, I enjoyed the latest ideas. I had mentors who believed in me and found me work at university. They made it as easy as possible for me to have a job and care for three small children. I did not have to choose between doing something for myself and something for others, as she did. And feminism had arrived, articulating a lot of my own feelings. I became filled with passion and she with defensiveness and a trace of bitterness, quickly suppressed. We saw more of each other but never discussed touchy or painful issues or intimate matters.

Then Dad died and Mum was alone. I watched her adjust to widowhood and saw a whole new side of her emerge. She joined clubs, made friends, went out more and became more outgoing, more tolerant and more relaxed. But it was almost too late, both for her and for our relationship. She was already 70, a life of hard work and worry had taken its toll, and her health gradually declined. In spending more time with her, I've come to see her strengths and to appreciate the characteristics we share. We're both stubborn, tenacious, strong-minded, independent and intelligent and we both enjoy a good laugh, although I don't remember Mum laughing much when I was young. I too have become more tolerant and less judgemental. I don't expect Mum to praise me or to take an interest in my work. I don't know what she thinks about me or what I do, and that's all right. I've also stopped blaming her for doing only what she believed in and had to do to survive. We've never been able to bridge the intimacy gap; deep feelings are left unspoken, personal matters and painful events are not discussed. I'm still sad at the lost opportunities, but I am no longer angry.

Instead, I enjoy the good things – the jokes, the outings, her sturdy independence and courage, the bright colours she wears and her appreciation of the time we have together. I see myself in her – I wonder what she would have done if she'd had the same opportunities – and I see lots of her in me. It is a rich and satisfying time, and I'm glad I've had it.

This relationship has been one of the most important and painful in my life. As I gradually made sense of it, I became curious about my friends' and colleagues' relationships with their mothers; I listened to women talk as part of my work; I brought up the subject at social gatherings. I was somewhat envious of women who described their mothers as their best friends, although others hissed through their teeth at the very mention of the word. It didn't take long to realise that whatever its nature, the mother-daughter relationship is invariably significant and intense.

I decided to investigate further. I was particularly interested in finding out how mothers and daughters keep their relationship going as their lives move along their separate paths. I was also interested in exploring the social changes that have made mothers' and daughters' life experiences very different. This book is the outcome of that research.

26 Mothers & Daughters

The two generations to which my mother and I belong have seen some major shifts in women's roles. There have been changes in work patterns: in 1951, only 18 per cent of all women were actively engaged in the paid labour force, but by 1990 that figure had risen to 63 per cent; in control of fertility, with the advent of the contraceptive pill; in social support, through the provision of welfare benefits; and in the law – women won the right to equal pay, although they are still clustered in a limited range of occupations, and discrimination on the grounds of sex has become illegal in a whole range of areas. Yet for all the changes, much remains the same. Women still bear the children and have most responsibility for caring for them; women also take the major responsibility for maintaining social links within families and provide the emotional glue that keeps families in touch, if not together. These personal connections make mother-daughter relationships as important now as in the past, although rapid social change may make them harder to maintain.

I decided to interview daughters aged between 30 and 45 and their mothers, although the book includes two exceptions to that rule. I wanted to talk to adult women who had had time to reflect on their own and their mothers' lives. The generations I chose are contiguous but very different: the daughters grew up after the war, their mothers were in the thick of it; the daughters grew up in a time of prosperity while their mothers grew up in the thirties Depression. Because I could include relatively few interviews, I limited myself to interviews with Pakeha women. To include one or two women from other cultures runs the risk of tokenism. My parents are thoroughly Pakeha and so am I, so it is not surprising that I feel most comfortable in Pakeha culture and want to understand it more.

I found some of my mothers and daughters through personal networks; others contacted me following early publicity about the book. I sought a good cross-section of backgrounds and experiences.

I wasn't looking for famous women, although it may be particularly interesting to investigate their relationships with their mothers. I was more interested in finding out how some 'ordinary' women managed their relationships with their mothers or their daughters. I was confident that any women I contacted would have a valuable story to tell – and so it proved. I spoke to rural women, city women, lesbians, single-parent mothers and / or daughters, women with good relationships with their mothers and women who had struggled to come to terms with difficulties. Sometimes my first contact was with the daughter, at other times with the mother, and mother or daughter negotiated agreement with the other half of the team. Usually I interviewed mothers and daughters separately, partly of necessity – few lived in the same city or town – and partly from choice, and the stories are presented one after the other. On two occasions I interviewed mother and daughter together and these interviews are reported as conversations.

In the interviews, I asked women to describe their own lives as well as commenting on their relationships with each other. This was partly to document differences in women's lives over the generations and partly to provide a context for their comments. For each of the women the emphasis was different: one story looks at a shift in dependence from mother to daughter, another at the impact of a daughter's demanding career on her relationship with her mother, several illustrate repeating patterns between mother and daughter, two discuss the effect of male violence and alcoholism on their relationship and two look at how the mothers reacted to their daughters' lesbianism. The stories are wide-ranging, and illustrate different styles of communicating and being, or not being, together.

The interviews were taped, transcribed and edited into a coherent story which I sent back to each person for confirmation or amendment. Very few people want to be represented in print by the first words to fall from their mouths, and women often added to or amended their stories by writing additions and correcting errors or deleting comments that were too painful or personal for public display or irrelevant to the story. Sometimes we taped second interviews and incorporated the new material into the story. The end result is a negotiated document which the women feel fairly represents what happened in their lives and in their relationships with each other. Some, particularly mothers, edited more than I would have liked, following my own mother's practice of not wanting to discuss anything painful or say anything that might be considered remotely boastful or self-promoting. I encouraged them to reinstate cuts; sometimes I was fully successful, at other times only moderately so. Either way, I feel confident that the finished products accurately reflect the women's characters and the relationships between them. I also encouraged the women to exchange manuscripts before they were finalised and most did this – the experience was sometimes painful or surprising and always interesting.

I appreciated the women's honesty and courage. They had to expose themselves first to me, then to their mother or daughter and finally to the world at large. Because some of their stories are painful and involve criticism of people close to them, some asked for anonymity. We decided that all the stories would be identified by a first name only, which the women chose. The book includes 10 pairs of mother-daughter stories, one set of stories from a mother and her two daughters, and three individual stories, all from daughters. One, now in her sixties, talks about her mother, now dead; another's mother is incapacitated, and the third has had a painful break with her mother over her sexuality.

Writing this book was a healing and rewarding task. I met 26 good women and listened to their journeys through life. I recognised many of the landmarks they described, and this increasing familiarity made my own journey easier. I learned that my experiences were neither unusual nor inevitable. I came to appreciate the good intent women have, their delight in each other's company and the support mothers and daughters can give each other 'in creating alternatives to values which tend to limit women's lives'.[1] Some of these alternatives are discussed in the conclusion along with the common threads that link these stories together. But now it is time to let the women speak for themselves.

1 Karen Payne, in Karen Payne (ed), *Between Ourselves: Letters Between Mothers and Daughters*, Houghton Mifflin Co., Boston, 1983.

Joan

Joan sets the scene for this book, identifying one of its main themes – the reticence and stoicism of our mothers' and grandmothers' generation and the resulting difficulty in communication. Her uncle once asked her, 'Did you ever really get to know your mother?', and she had to say, 'No'.

Joan is something of an anomaly in this book – she is of the mothers' generation but tells a daughter's story. She and her daughter and grand-daughter live near each other in the country, but her daughter was not ready to talk about Joan. She acknowledged sadly that there are still obstacles to communication between the generations.

Joan

I was born in Featherston on 7 August 1928 in Nurse Abbot's nursing home – people went to nursing homes in those days – and the nurse used to knock the mothers out with chloroform before they gave birth. Mum never knew what it was like to have a baby till she had my brother Andrew in a hospital two and a half years later.

Mum brought me home to no hot water and a black coal range. The house was made up of two cottages joined together. They were built for the military in about 1865, and it was the pokiest, miserablest little thing, with a tank outside the door, a pit toilet down in the laurel trees and a pump to get your water. The washing was done in an old shed outside – no taps, you had to hump the water first from the pump, and there was a scrubbing board and copper.

Mum and Dad always had a magnificent garden and she was always trying to make good things for us but I can remember one day we only had pumpkins and onions to eat. How terrible for her. She had been crying, I realise now, but you didn't hear her grumbling. She never said anything, she made the best of it to us kids. She was very forward when it came to food and fresh air. We always had open windows at night. And when brown bread came out in 1936 or so she used to buy it. And she made plenty of salads.

She was one of those ladies who always loved having the place smelling nice. She wasn't fanatical but she would polish all the floors and she always had soup or something like that boiling on the stove. She was always knitting – unpicking and knitting – and undoing clothes and turning them inside out. Think of doing that to a coat. Making sack pinnies for the morning and nice flourbag pinnies for the afternoon fancy-worked with flowers. I've still got pinnies she embroidered for me when I was little.

I can remember the day we got the radio and the joy of dancing to the music. Mum used to bake every Saturday and she'd say, 'Get outside, you kids, you know I'm baking, I'm busy.' And out we'd go but she used to bake and listen to football on this radio.

She had a great sense of humour. She'd make us laugh when

things went wrong. She'd cuddle us but she'd laugh until the tears ran down her face because she could see the funny side and of course in the end we'd laugh too. She'd say, 'Come on now, there's worse things happen at sea.' She was incredible for sayings – 'You've got a lip like a motherless foal', or 'I'll knock you half way into next week', or 'Black as the inside of a cow'.

She had two lady friends – they always called each other 'Mrs' – they were bosom pals and they used to play cards together. Once a week they would come to each other's houses and play casino – it's a card game. So every second week she wasn't there when we got home. That to me was the end of the world, to walk in without Mum. Of course she'd be home in next to no time, she wasn't far away, and she would leave a little treat – icing sugar and butter made into a little lolly.

Mum never said 'love' or 'dear' or anything like that. The strongest thing she'd say was 'lovey'. Your world was made if Mum said 'lovey' – which was very rarely. And she didn't believe in telling us we were pretty, that would not have been right. But she loved us and we were safe with Mum.

When I was about eight we shifted to a sheep station. It was absolute bliss. We could go for miles and miles in the bush and round the private lake. It was great. We blossomed, even Mum blossomed. Just imagine, hot water in the taps!

But she never told me anything about menstruation or sex or anything like that. Once a woman came to stay in Matt's whare, a pig shooter's wife. I thought she was a strange little round lady, but I heard some grown-up say, 'She's having a baby.' So I ran home and said, 'Mrs Ball's having a baby.' I think I got a clip around the ears because that would have meant sex, and you don't mention it – it mustn't even be thought of or whispered or hinted at. So I was clipped round the ears and told, 'Now get outside and mind your own business.'

Mum always used to get in a flap when anything like that came up so it was never talked about, and when I was 12 I knew nothing. I had two older sisters – they didn't say anything to me either. Even though there were cows around giving birth, Mum and Dad used to sidle us off from that too. Dad rather thought that girls should be above those sorts of things. We weren't allowed to say 'blimey' or anything like that because we were girls. I was 11 and Mum well and truly round and pregnant. I still didn't realise, even when she went off mysteriously to hospital.

One day when I was 12 I made my bed. I didn't usually, but maybe I thought I'd give Mum a surprise. I made it and went tripping and singing across the paddock and over to the chook house to feed my chooks. Mum, ever suspicious, must have shot in there and looked in my bed. Evidently there was a drip which I hadn't noticed or thought of, and to my horror when I got back – look, I'm going hot and cold thinking of it – she ripped me away into the bedroom, talking ninety to the dozen. She pulled my pants down – I was aghast and embarrassed at what was going on – and ripped a bit of rag into my pants, pulled them up and said, 'Now you've got your period. You're unwell. This is what happens to girls.' Well, I survived it. I know I went around wondering about this astonishing lump of rag in there. She made me a little bit of elastic to keep it up. I survived that and just took it in my stride.

We went up to Featherston School for a while, 50 miles a day in all, but hated it. I remember one day we went over to the boss's big sheds and got a whole lot of little tacks – we were desperate – and put them all across the road. The bus just whizzed over them and nothing happened! So it wasn't very long before Mum said, 'You're going to have Correspondence School, you're going to have school at home.' That was lovely. We had a little school room in the whare and we made it all nice and pretty. It had a fireplace and everything. That's where we did our school work. We had to do it from 9 to 12 and 1 to 3 and all that.

But I let school fizzle after a while. I was 16 and I was taking up dress designing. They told me I had tremendous potential but I just wanted to get out on my horse and gallop around the hills, and I did. That just shows you how mad I was. In the war Mum and my sister Grace made camouflage nets and they used to knit masses of little jerseys and balaclavas and socks and all these things. But I never did – I was out into the hills and away and away.

I realise now I would have made a great engineer. I loved water and roads and all that sort of thing. Mum and Dad should have encouraged it. But they never really encouraged us for anything. Mum did what was right and brought us up straight and proper as best she could, to be honest, decent and clean. She was pretty tight with the money and it would have been expensive. She wouldn't have liked that. She thought we would get married, that was the thing. Get married, which for me was a disaster. We should have done much more.

As the war advanced and the blokes were going away we'd have dances at the school to say hooray to them, and Mum and Dad would always take us. They were absolutely marvellous dances – Hector Smith on the violin and the blacksmith's wife on piano. I loved them. We'd talk about them for days beforehand and days afterwards. Sometimes we'd have a dance at our place and Mum would clear all the furniture out of the sitting room and make sure the linoleum was all polished. We'd help because we were keen. Then Mum would set to and bake. For music, Dad would play his accordion or mouth organ. I still have them. Oh, they were wonderful times, sneaked kisses and all that sort of thing.

When I was about 17, there was a dance on for the soldiers in Featherston and somehow I kidded Mum and Dad to let me go up there. Well, I was a country bumpkin, no doubt about that. I crept in there. I had no idea I was lovely and attractive, none whatsoever, not really. I thought I had a nice little waist, but the first fellow I saw was the one I married. It became a habit and in due course he beguiled me into his bed. I found what passion was about, that's all it was, and thought, 'This is it. I'll marry him.' And that's what it was all about.

I was 19 when I married. I didn't have to get married but I got a baby at once. Nine months after I was married, I had Lance. The marriage was a failure, it was awful.

Mum was thankful we were getting married, I know that. They gave all of us a lovely wedding as best they could. The wedding days were good days. Mum said, 'I would have thought you would marry a farmer', and I remember the tone of her voice – sad. And I had a niggle. I knew it was wrong. I knew it was passion, that's all it was.

We rubbed along and did our best and I tried never to fight in front of the kids or at Mum and Dad's. Hide it all, have a good happy clean home, do the best you can: that was the way. I lived over in the Hutt and Mum was in Featherston. But I didn't want to burden her anyway. She'd had all of us and I would never have told her, never, never – my pride. Anyway she wouldn't have understood. She would have said, 'Well, you've made your bed, you have to lie in it. You knew what you were doing. If you didn't you're old enough now, old enough and ugly enough to know what you're doing.' That sort of thing.

When I was 35, Julie was eight, Roger was four and Lance, the eldest, had left home, my husband had gone out and I'd gone to bed. I heard funny draggy footsteps coming in and I knew instantly he'd had a stroke. He staggered into bed and I rang up dear old Dr Milne and he rushed around and they took him to hospital. He was dead in a month. It was a release. I felt sorry for him but it was good being free again.

I got the widow's benefit. The only money I had was £200, because the only money I ever got apart from a bit of food money was child allowance and I made the absolute most of that allowance. I gathered myself together and got myself into a system. I got over the shock of the whole ghastly thing, then I started to look around, to begin again.

Every single weekend, Saturday or Sunday, I'd come and see Mum and Dad, Julie and me. I'd come over the hill and maybe go out with Dad. He used to love driving in the countryside and as he got older he couldn't drive. I always got on well with Mum but she would never ever confide her feelings or her thoughts. You kept that from the kids. And she was terribly brave because she had very bad veins, always did have. I remember her hurrying around doing the work with her veins all done up with bandages, round and round and round. She never believed in crying in front of you or anything like that.

After Dad died in 1977, she really packed up. To her horror she became incontinent. I couldn't have her at my place because I had a ghastly outside toilet and Mum couldn't walk, except for hobbling a little bit. I had a job and I'd come over as much as I could, but it was all very depressing. It was sad, so she ended up in the Greytown Hospital old people's place, which she hated. One day she said so wistfully to me, 'What will become of my little treasures?' That still makes me cry.

I could never really talk to her, not about anything heartfelt. I think it would embarrass her and worry her. I would never have told her any worries because she'd say, 'Oh well, come on, you've got to buck up, go and make the best of it', but she would really worry. So I never ever did talk to her.

I remember when I'd had Lance, I bled for five months on and off. I realise now they should have done something. I'd come over from the Hutt to visit Mum, which I did as often as I could. I was standing by her fireplace, and I had a clot which went 'tuh' down on the hearth. I was aghast. It slipped out, got away, and Mum was horrified. Couldn't cope with it. So I couldn't let her really know, I had to make the best of it and laugh the matter off and clean it up. But I felt pretty crook. So I couldn't share at that level.

Mum was starved for love, starved for attention, especially when she was young. She was only 18 when she married; Dad was 34. Dad was kind and loving and good but when it came to women he wouldn't have known what made them tick, apart from always having the wood in the box and a garden and never hitting or anything.

Upon reflection I realise Mum always had a hard bitterness when it came to love. If a young married couple called each other 'darling' or were loving, Mum would go sort of stiff and prim and disapproving and say, 'It's time they got over that.' Anyway, it spanked of sex which obviously made her very uncomfortable and somehow reminded her of her own lack of fulfilment.

She did have some sort of birth control. Once she sent me to her room and I saw a drawer half open and within was a glass tube-like bottle with largish tablets with maybe a couple gone. I didn't touch, but by the words on it I realise now it was some kind of birth control tablet.

Once Dad said wistfully how he'd like to see Mum in black stockings. How sad. She would never have done so. Her abiding fear was that one of her girls would 'get into trouble'. Once I discovered the joys of flirting she looked upon me as always on the brink of shaming the family.

Yet apart from her hidden frustrations she was open and fun and a great Mum. We had lovely Christmases and birthdays. When visitors came there was fun, laughter and music, delightful camping holidays and picnics. But of her inner self, no one ever knew. Once her half-brother said to me, 'Did you ever really get to know your mother?' and I said, 'No.' 'None of us ever did either,' he said.

She taught us to respect our elders, to fear God ('He can see you'), to be honest, to work with a will, to save and not to speak ill of the dead. She was better than I could ever be.

Marie & Joanne

The lives of Marie and Joanne reflect the changes between the generations that grew up during the war and the one that grew up after it.

Although her mother died when she was young, Marie had already absorbed her family's strong Catholic beliefs and values, particularly regarding the sacredness of marriage and the importance of the family. In accordance with the custom of the time, she left work as soon as she married and stayed home to care for her seven daughters and one son.

In contrast, Joanne lives with her partner in a committed but secular relationship rather than a marriage, and as a qualified lawyer and a feminist, juggles childcare and a career.

There is one rather ironic 'anomaly' in their relationship. Joanne would like her mother to be a more traditional grandmother, while Marie is enjoying having time to herself and an independent adult life! But despite their different experiences, Marie and Joanne have a strong bond and respect each other's achievements.

Marie

I come from a farming family in the Waikato and one of my first memories of my mother is the day she enrolled me at the Te Aroha Convent school. I'll never forget that day because she made me wear gloves. I said to her, 'Why do I have to wear gloves?', and she answered, 'Because the Sisters are ladies.' I thought that epitomised my mother – I always remember her as a lady.

She died when I was just 12. I remember coming home from school and she would often be resting. One day when I came home everyone was tip-toeing around and she was in bed. She'd had a stroke. I was allowed to go in and say good night, then sent next door. When I came back the next morning she was dead. That was all fairly traumatic.

Phyl, my older sister, did her best to fill the gap but then she went off to travel and get married. I was sent to boarding school and a lot of my life was spent coming home to housekeepers who were not really interested in a teenager arriving home in the holidays and ruffling the routine. I was always trying not to be a nuisance. On the other hand, I think I was probably very indulged because Dad and my brothers felt a bit guilty about me. I was allowed to drive a car and in those days that was really quite something. I was never without anything. I was sent to university with all my expenses paid.

When I finished school, I think everybody looked for something that would keep me occupied. They chose what was considered a safe degree – home science. I don't remember ever being asked about it and I don't think I had any other expectations myself. I was quite happy to go along with it and it seemed very exciting to go to Dunedin. I think they chose home science because it was suitable and it got me out of the way for another three years and they hoped at the end of it I'd move on to something else.

Well, as it happened I moved on to meeting Maurice. We were engaged when I completed the degree and married a few months later, so I really did do the right thing by them all!

I would have been happy to have gone for a job, and I was looking to go into either teaching or dietetics. I was trying to decide which, but once I met Maurice – it was one of those instant fall-in-love jobs and it's never changed. I graduated in November and the marriage was set for April. I had to do all the arrangements myself, absolutely everything. I was at home on my own with Dad, so that kept me busy. Neither family expected for one minute that I would work – it just wasn't done. I married a lawyer and lawyers' wives didn't work. Anyway, it was a lovely challenge having a house of my own, and within 12 months Joanne arrived so there was never time to get restless. From then on, as you can imagine, with eight children I was busy.

Natural family planning was the only means of birth control acceptable to us, and natural family planning really had more mistakes than anything else in it, but it didn't worry us. We wanted a big family of about four or five, maybe six, but after five, all of whom were girls, Andrew arrived as our first son. That was lovely, but then we thought it was a bit selfish for Andrew to be on his own, so we had one more. Of course we had another daughter, but that was really it. Six years later when I found I was pregnant it seemed a disaster. Nikki, our seventh daughter, and I often joke about how unwanted she was.

We were reasonably relaxed about having daughters but by about the fourth there was a little bit of a concern, mainly because of the pressure from others. Other people felt sorry for Maurice not having a son and I began to feel a little bit inadequate, then I read all about genetics and realised it wasn't me. When we did have a son, of course we were thrilled. 'Thank God everybody else will get off our backs,' we agreed.

Joanne was the eldest. I probably fussed more over her than the others, but without a mother I was really on my own. Maurice's mother was alive and I don't suppose any daughter-in-law and mother-in-law have the perfect relationship. Although she never interfered with me I couldn't understand that she didn't want to be more interested in the children, and she certainly didn't want to do any caring for them. She liked to see them for perhaps half an hour – have them brought in and taken away – but she loved them dearly in her own way and she bought wonderful presents for them. But she didn't want to get involved, so I was on my own. Now I'm a grandmother myself I can better understand how she felt.

I've never had any problem with role relationships – I just did it. I had cleaning help from about the second or third child on, and I had a Karitane nurse for two weeks each time I came home from the hospital. We stayed in the hospital longer in those days, we weren't in and out: it was 10 days of luxury hotel treatment. So I came home fairly rested. We didn't go out much either. When we met our friends, they came for dinner at home or we went to their places.

When the children were young they all went to the local convent school. Looking back, it all seems very easy. I know there must have been a lot of work, and that was okay because I was happy, but there weren't issues. Even when Joanne went off to Baradene College for her secondary education she seemed happy and I don't remember any issues. Maybe it was because there weren't the options. It was a toll call to Auckland so the girls didn't talk for hours on the phone. They didn't go out with boyfriends. Dating wasn't accepted. The big social event was the school dance and that was highly supervised. Probably by today's standards she was over-protected. I don't know whether that was good or bad for her but it was the way it was done then. The issues didn't arise until much later, after university really and when she was starting work.

We expected them all to go to university. It's just the way of life of our backgrounds and they are academically able. I can't remember how Joanne came to choose law – three of them have. I don't know if we pressured them. I would like to think that we have allowed them to make their choices. In bringing them up, the most important thing to us was that they be in a disciplined environment that led them to self-discipline and allowed them to move from there to freedom. Not freedom from, but freedom to get on and make their own choices, their own decisions and their own way of life. When they actually did it, we didn't always like the things they did, so the freedom backfired on us in some ways, but that's life, isn't it?

Joanne went down to Otago University. I think because they'd had years of spending hours travelling to school in the city, they hadn't had an opportunity to build up friendships. I felt in some ways they lost out on that side of it. So we thought that it would be really good for her to have the opportunity to mix with students her own age. She began in a hostel, then went flatting. We thought, 'That's really going to be good for her', and that set the trend. I wouldn't like to think that one of our children missed out because of the many others, but it certainly made it easier to let them go their own way because I had so much else to think about. There were 15 years between Joanne and Nikki, so I was reluctantly looking after another baby while Jo was at university. I didn't want to get too involved with her. I just enjoyed the thought that she was moving on and that she was okay. I didn't have any worries about it because I'd done it at much the same age.

We have been very lucky. We've had no major worry as regards drugs, drink, teenage suicide or what in the seventies was a huge fear for most mothers – an unwanted pregnancy. We haven't had to face any of those issues. Whether I was just very complacent in thinking that we wouldn't, whether we've just been plain lucky, or whether we did give them the value system to carry them through, I don't know.

We could talk about most things, although one of the hang-ups was sex education because it was a big deal. I always used to think that because I worked with Marriage Guidance as a family life tutor and went round schools for a few years that I was pretty good at it. Looking back on it, I don't know that I was that brilliant. I think I gave them things to read and answered anything they asked, but particularly after Joanne and Jenny, I just let them learn from one another. I can remember opening up a drawer and finding birth-control pills and being pretty shocked and thinking 'My goodness!', then thinking, 'Well, they must know enough to know that this is what they want to do, so okay.' I think possibly because of my upbringing and traditional reticence it was hard and I'm not sure whether we did it very well. But they don't seem to have had any problems from it.

When Joanne finished university, she came back home and worked up at the office. Then it was time for the overseas experience and I think that this is when things first got a little heated. Before she went to England she'd met Peter, who is now her partner. They went overseas and I'm pretty sure they travelled together. We were a bit shocked by this but it was out of sight so it didn't put any of us on the spot. When they came back she said that she and Peter were going to live together. Well, that was the first real ruction in our house and I cannot for the life of me imagine why it was, because now I don't even think about it. Today I really don't see it as an issue but then it was, and we felt as if we had failed somehow to give them an understanding of the importance of marriage and commitment. They saw marriage and commitment from a different perspective. They didn't necessarily see formal marriage as being important or even as the only way to show commitment, but we did. And oh, it was a very hard time. She was in tears, I was in tears – it was a trying time. But they did it. They lived together.

About a year later they moved into a property of their own. I had an inkling that there may be going to be a pregnancy, and both families put considerable pressure on them to make some public commitment. Peter is Jewish and people said, 'Well, if they marry, will they marry in the Catholic church or would they marry in a Jewish synagogue, or could they?' I said, 'It doesn't really matter as long as they just do something.' I wouldn't have cared if they'd married on the moon, quite frankly. It got to the stage where none of us talked about it. Then they told us about a partnership agreement and gave it to us to read. It was a great relief. Jo and Peter had a party at their place, invited both families and their friends, drank a bottle of champagne and signed their partnership agreement. It's not a marriage in a church, it's not a marriage in a synagogue, but it's commitment and that made us happy, and very soon Hugo was on the way. I have a suspicion that they didn't want to face both parents with a pregnancy as well as living together, so the agreement was their answer.

Now I see Joanne and Peter living an excellent-value life. You couldn't label it Catholic or Jewish but they care deeply for one another and they live life according to the family values that they grew up with, so it's okay.

The other issue is being a grandmother. I hate being a grandmother. At least with having children the decision is your own – not that I ever did it very well! – but you can't decide about having grandchildren. They just arrive on you and you're supposed to love it. Everybody says, 'Are you a grandmother yet?', and when you say, 'Yes', they say, 'How wonderful for you.' But I don't agree. Because I had so many children myself, I'm sure I OD'd on little ones. Now I want friends. After 30 years I have at last got to the stage where my children are adult friends, and now I'm back to having pre-schoolers and babies that I'm supposed to have this wonderful grandmotherly love for. This is an issue with Jo and I particularly, although it possibly is with the others too but they're not as vocal as she is. I've explained to her that at this stage I feel I need time out – time just to do what I feel like doing and not to feel I've got to be an adoring grandmother. She understands that and intellectually she accepts it, but emotionally it's been an issue. She was very hurt and expressed her hurt. I found it really hard to respond so I wrote to her about it, because I find it's easier to express my feelings in writing. When she read the letter, she said, 'Mum, you know it's just what you said before. I understand that, but you've always brought us up to think that a family is important and I just can't quite see how you can be like this.' So it is a bit of an issue, but I'm finding it easier as the children get older and they become people. My own children have never asked me to look after their babies. They accept that I'm not going to do that, but they just want me to be a bit more interested. So I'm working on it and I think it will come, but I just feel that I haven't had enough time between being a full-time mother and a grandmother. Nikki only left home to go flatting last year.

There's an unbelievable difference between the way the girls run their lives and the way I ran mine. The expectation when I left university was that if you married a lawyer you didn't work. It was almost a slight on your husband if you worked. But Joanne was a lawyer marrying a lawyer and naturally she didn't expect that her career would be any less or any different from his. So the difference between us is quite extraordinary.

In some ways Joanne is like me. She has the same enjoyment of people. She likes talking with people and she's pretty straight from the shoulder. I think that for better or worse so am I. She's academically able; I'm not top academic but I'm academically able and her father was too, of course. I think we are rather alike and that probably put a bit of pressure on her. I've never found it difficult to talk and relate with her. The first one they say is the hardest, but not for me. She always says she had quite a bit of pressure put on her because she was the eldest. I am sure it did happen but I was unaware of it. Perhaps it's an automatic thing that happens to the eldest child. She says that she had to break all the rules so that others could do it and not get the backfire that she got.

But I had to laugh the other day. I said, 'We didn't consciously think about it, but we always thought that you would do what we thought you should do. It was quite a shock when you didn't.' And she said, 'Well, that's exactly what I think about Hugo and Rosa. Of course they'll want to do what I think they *should*.' And I thought, 'Perhaps it's natural.' Because there she is having made a whole change between her life and mine and yet she probably isn't any more prepared to face the fact that it could happen to her than I was.

I expect each of them to do as they choose within their partnership set-up. I don't care what they do – I just want to see them as fulfilled women. I didn't expect for one minute that Joanne wouldn't want to continue work as a lawyer. In fact, I'd have been quite mortified if she stayed home – all that education, all those opportunities – which is not to say that I see home as a second-rate situation. For me it's been a fulfilment because I've been able to do a lot of things and I haven't had the monetary pressure. Most women couldn't afford to stay home today, even if they wanted to. My daughters vary in the degree that they follow their careers, depending on their other commitments. But I think they have more pressure on them than I did because in some ways society expects them to get on with their dual home and careers, whereas I didn't have that expectation placed on me. Maurice and I had roles which were absolutely defined. Within that definition we worked together perfectly.

Do I wish I'd had the opportunities they have? I've thought about that and I'm not sure. I know that I've been happy with the way life turned out for me and I wouldn't want it changed, but I wouldn't mind a second go to find out if it would be any better!

I think I've become rather selfish since the family left. I tend to talk about what they want to talk about, but I'm not living my life through them. I'm not wanting to probe into their lives. I might be kidding myself – maybe I'm a really interfering busybody and don't know it. But I don't want their problems. I'm happy if they're happy, leading their lives, fulfilled in them and we keep in touch and are friends. That's enough. Maybe the time will come when I will enter into a lonely phase and drive them mad trying to live my life through them. But at the moment I just want them to get on with it and leave me to get on with mine.

They know that we're always here for them. Not just me, because Maurice and I have a very good marriage. He is not as involved in their everyday lives but he's a very loving father and very supportive of them.

To me a family is a wonderful part of life – I couldn't imagine life without a family. Wherever they are, we always keep in contact. Even when they're travelling they'll phone in every few months. And we've never had periods when we haven't talked to any one of them, never. They have never ever had a major fight that I know of, and they're all interested in one another and friends. I'm wondering if I'm allowed to sound pleased with myself about that. Yes, I think I'll permit myself to say I am. I feel that has been an achievement. Sometimes after watching all the wonderful things that women do with their careers, I think, 'Well, all I've been is a wife and mother. Is it enough?' Then I look round and see all these independent people living good, fulfilling lives and I think, 'Yes, it's been really worthwhile.'

Joanne

It's hard to remember way back to my childhood, but it was happy and we always had good family holidays. With eight children in the family there were always kids around and it was really busy. I was the eldest and I remember being responsible for other members of the family. Mum and Dad organised the four oldest of us to look after the four youngest – we were responsible for getting them up in the morning, getting them dressed, making the beds, that sort of thing. I felt I had quite a lot of responsibility growing up, and I don't know whether Mum really appreciated that. Maybe that's just the way it works in big families. I'm sure now, having had two kids, that you couldn't do it any other way.

Mum was incredibly organised. We always had lunch at the same time, dinner at the same time, everybody had their jobs to do. But within that we had free time and lots of talking with both our parents, but particularly with Mum. As a mother, she was always there for us. God knows how she managed it with eight kids, but she was brilliant, always there. Dad was too but Mum was the communicator in the family, as Mums often are, I suppose.

We were brought up quite strictly. Mum and Dad always had to meet anybody I was going out with and we always had to be home at definite times. They were very strict about that. We were only allowed to go out maybe one night a week and it was really controlled. If we were going to a party they would drive us – that was when we were young and still at school.

I went to Baradene College. It was a Catholic school but there was quite a strong liberal streak running through it when I was there, certainly in my class. It exposed us to lots of different things that we maybe weren't exposed to at home. It was liberal Catholicism, which in a way was how Mum and Dad brought us up.

I was always in the A stream but I don't think the choice of subjects was that great really. I did straight sciences. I don't know what input my parents had in that decision but I did maths, physics, biology and chemistry in the fifth, sixth and seventh forms. When

I got into the seventh form I hated physics and chemistry and couldn't believe that I'd chosen to do sciences.

I had been going to go to Massey University to do a food technology degree – that's what I'd wanted to do – but I changed to arts. Trying to decide what to do was really difficult because Mum and Dad weren't keen on us doing 'just a BA'. They wanted us to do a degree that would qualify us for something. I was interested in law and could combine it with arts, so that is what I did. There was never any question about my going to university – it was expected.

As for choosing universities – the Otago campus had a great reputation and quite a few of my friends were going there. I decided if I went to Auckland University I would continue in the same kind of clique and I would probably have to live at home. I think I would have qualified for boarding and bursary allowances, but home would have been right there as well and I really wanted to get away. I don't think we missed out on anything as kids – I had my own bedroom, so I had privacy – but I really wanted to get away from home and be by myself rather than be part of eight kids. So I chose to go to Otago, and it was great, I loved it. I really enjoyed being there.

In my first year I was incredibly homesick for the first couple of terms. It was my first time away from home and I was desperate to get home in the May holidays – I think Mum was really pleased to see me as well. After I'd been away for two years I suddenly thought my parents were okay, that my mother wasn't as bad as I thought she was! I began to appreciate the home life that I had and what they had provided for us. It was the usual thing, I suppose – as soon as you leave home you realise what you've had.

I transferred to Auckland for the last year of my degree and worked in my father's firm for the year I did my Professionals. At the end of that year I decided I wanted to travel. I wanted to get away from law and have a complete break, so I went to do some skiing and travelling around the States. I worked as a waitress to finance the travel.

I think Mum and Dad realised that I was going to do it and they never said they weren't happy about it. Mum was really good like that, she always listened to what I — what all of us — had to say. You could bounce ideas off her and discuss them with her and she'd always have a definite view which she would give you. But she didn't seem too concerned about me wanting to travel at that time. She and Dad always monitored us while we were away in quite a good way. After I had been there for a year, I wanted to stay on longer and the woman I went with came back to New Zealand to get married. She wanted me to return for the wedding, but I didn't have the money to pay for the tickets. My parents offered me a return ticket.

As soon as I came home I remember having lots of discussions and Mum and Dad whisking me away to the bach at the Mount after the wedding. We had some serious talks about where I was going and was I going to practise law and why was I going back to the States and hadn't I already been there long enough? They'd given me the return ticket so I knew I had the option to go back, and I'd left all my stuff there. I think that both Mum and Dad were really good at that time because they realised I was probably drifting a bit, and that if I didn't get some experience in law then it would become more difficult for me to practise. They didn't actually say, 'We think you should stay', but they certainly gave the very strong feeling that that was what they thought. They gave me a few options and a few ideas to consider and Mum was really good. I really thank them now for doing that, because it was definitely the right move for me to come back at that point and start practising law. I stayed, cancelled my return ticket and had my stuff shipped home.

Mum's always been really good at assessing the individual needs of each of us – amazing considering she's got eight children. I haven't always agreed with her decisions but I have agreed with a lot of them.

I stayed here for nearly three years and worked as a lawyer. It was during that time that I met Peter and we got together. We went out together for a year and then I decided that I wanted to live with him, but I knew that was going to be a big deal for Mum and Dad because they were very keen on the concept of marriage. We'd been brought up in a very Catholic way and marriage was definitely expected. I didn't want to get married – I didn't believe in marriage – so I had to tell them I'd decided to live with Peter. And it was terrible, absolutely dreadful. They were very upset about it. They did everything they could to talk me out of it. Both of them. There were lots of tears. But I was really determined that was what I was going to do, even if they didn't agree with it. They've certainly changed their views now. Once they got to about number three or four, it was just so much easier for them.

Two years later Peter and I decided to travel. We wanted to spend six months travelling through Asia to England and then to live and work as solicitors in London. This resulted in another family crisis. Travelling and working in London was okay, but not as an 'unmarried couple'. At this stage I think my parents accepted that they couldn't stop me and instead of the fierce arguments there was tense discussion and much sadness on their part.

We never did get married. We decided that it wasn't really the right thing for us. It's not so much an issue now but it was when we came back four or five years ago. Both Mum and Dad really did want us to get married and so did Peter's parents. It was very difficult to explain why we didn't want to get married and to get that through.

I think there are two reasons for getting married. Either you get married for religious reasons under the eyes of God, or, if you're not religious, for the civil ceremony and the fact that you contract to the state, and neither of those two seemed relevant to us really. We'd decided that we wanted to be together and we'd made a really strong personal commitment to each other and we didn't feel the need to have a ceremony.

In retrospect I can see why the public side of it can be quite a positive thing because it's good for the families to get together and for everybody to recognise and to be happy about the commitment, but we chose not to do that because we believed it was a personal matter. We'd decided what we wanted and we didn't believe that there would be any problem as far as our children were concerned. With both of us being lawyers we knew what the law was – our children were protected if we had any problems — and property was something we knew we would want to cover with a contract because de facto relationships are not covered by the Matrimonial Property Act.

At this stage in my life, I was fed up with the fact that my parents were constantly disappointed by my actions. I was a practising solicitor, I was in a good relationship and I was pregnant, and I thought I'd done everything okay really. But they definitely didn't and Peter's parents were really upset about the fact that we weren't getting married. We had already decided to have a property contract. We expanded the contract to include other issues such as any children that we might have and called it a marriage contract. We drafted up our own contract, invited our parents and family and close friends to our place and sat down and signed it in front of them. We told them what it meant for us, then went out to dinner with the two families, which was good because it made everybody realise that we actually were serious about our relationship. They could almost say we were married. Since then I think that Mum has definitely accepted our relationship and she views us as married. But for us there was an important distinction. We did not buy the whole traditional concept of marriage and husbands and wives. I particularly did not want to be a wife and I didn't want to be called Mrs. I wanted to retain my own individuality as much as possible.

Later came the issue of grandchildren. I think when kids go off and leave home in their late teens and early twenties they don't really want to have much to do with their parents. They're sorting out what they want with their own lives, so maybe that's a break between the child and the parent. But when you come back and have your own children, you want that contact back. I wanted Mum to be involved in what I was doing and in what the children were doing. I didn't want her to be there to look after them like a lot of grandmothers do, but I definitely wanted her to be around. I wanted to be able to discuss things with her. I have been able to do that to a certain extent, but not nearly as much as I want because she's now got her own life. She has her own interests. She's got her friends and the freedom to do the things that she wants to do – bridge, golf and so on. She's even managed to start writing. I think it's really brilliant to have the confidence to do that. I know just from being out of the workforce for a year or two how it knocks your confidence, so I really admire her achievements in her writing. She was probably unable to do that for many years because of her involvement with the kids. But I would like her to be more available. I'd like her to see the kids more. They adore her, they're always talking about her, so there's definitely a relationship there, but I'd just like her to be around a bit more. I've talked to her about it, but not very much because it's still quite a difficult subject. It will probably change as the children get older and as her life changes.

Our lives have been very similar in that we both had partners and we both have children, but different in that I had a career which I've pursued. She had one too but didn't ever get a chance to pursue it because she began to have children when she was 21. It wasn't really accepted then for women to do anything except raise children. It must have been hell. In a way it was simpler in those days, because your choices were really limited – you either pursued your career or got married and had kids. Now we try to do both. I established my career before I had children and I've tried to maintain it since. I am finding the balancing act very difficult.

I think Mum and I are quite similar in other ways, too. We are both fairly forthright. We have opinions on things and we are not afraid to speak out about things that we believe are important. Mum's approach has always been: if there's a problem, deal with it, discuss it and resolve it – and I think I'm like that too. I can't stand things being left.

The way I bring up my children is going to be completely different from the way I was brought up, partly because I'm not going to be there all the time in the same way Mum was. But I think my values are very similar to my parents', although Mum and Dad have Catholicism as a reason for their values and I don't. We were brought up with a Catholic background, with strong morals and really good, basic, caring values, and I think that I have those same values and will probably bring up my kids with those values. But it may be more difficult for me to pass them on. Brought up with Catholicism, there was always a reason why you had to care or be honest – God was always there. I don't have that same reason to give to my children.

Feminism has affected my whole life. When I went to university in the seventies feminism had just started. I've always been involved in women's organisations. Mum and I always talked about it. When I was younger she would almost go the other way, take the opposite viewpoint to bring me to some balanced level, I suppose. In retrospect, when I see the way she's lived her life and what she's like now, she's a real feminist. She's very much an independent woman with her own thoughts and views and always has been and we've been brought up like that. It's just that I guess she tried to balance my views a bit. I think she probably thinks much the same as I do about women. I'm sure that if she hadn't had eight children and hadn't been in the position that she was in, she would have lived her life quite differently.

The difference between us is the church. All those issues that came out when I was at school and in my earlier years at university – like abortion, marriage, contraception, all those issues that the Catholic church said no to – she always accepted the church's view. And I always took the opposite view. Which is why I couldn't really ever accept Catholicism – to me the church seems so incredibly backward. I know that it has been a big disappointment to her that we did not choose to live as Catholics and we haven't christened our children.

Mum's a really good communicator. She's also open to new ideas, which I think has a lot to do with the fact that she's had seven daughters and one son. She's had to deal with so many issues, she's definitely softened her style a bit. The communication lines between us are very open. I talk to my friends about things that I probably wouldn't talk to her about — I still think of her as my mother — but I'm still able to talk to her about almost anything.

She's always there to talk to on the phone – if she's got time. She tends to deal with the children who need her. If there's somebody who's got a problem, she will concentrate on that, which is understandable because her time is more limited, but there are often things I want to talk to her about but I'm not able to because she hasn't got the time. In a way she's repeating the same pattern she had. Her mother was dead and she had no help from her mother-in-law. Mum often said to me, 'I had no help with you kids, there was nobody I could turn to and that was really difficult.' It's almost like she's doing the same thing, but perhaps not quite to the same extent.

Peggy & Jane

I interviewed Peggy and Jane together in the house which they have shared for over a year. I was curious to know how they came to live together and how well the arrangement worked. It didn't take long to find out that it worked very well indeed. The interview was punctuated with laughter, moments of empathy and understanding, queries and responses, as each listened to the other, and occasionally elaborated a point.

Peggy married young when she was pregnant. She was ill-prepared for marriage, but in an era of stoicism and silence, was expected to cope. With no women's refuges and no Matrimonial Property Act, it was many years before she could leave her violent and abusive husband.

Jane also married young and expected things to be different. They weren't, but she left sooner than her mother. It wasn't long before her son began to be violent too. He is now in boarding school and the two women live in peace.

Their story is an example of a cycle of repeating patterns broken by a creative solution.

Peggy and Jane

PEGGY: My mother and father and my paternal grandparents had all come out from England after the First World War and we all lived very close by, in Hamilton. I have one brother who is 12 months older than I am but I was always in the same class as him at school. I grew up with the impression that I wasn't very bright and it wasn't until later on that I realised that it wasn't that I wasn't bright, it was just that I was a year younger and less mature than the others. In my third year of high school we moved to Auckland, which was fatal for my education because I had to go to another secondary school where I didn't know a soul. I was totally at sea, so at the end of my third year I left and went into business college, although I had always said I would never work in an office. But I took to the shorthand and typing like a duck to water. I was only there nine months before I went to work at about 18 bob a week. I lived at home and got a job in a government office – the routine thing.

My parents didn't expect anything of me, partly because my mother had had to leave school when she was nine – she could read and write very well, but beyond that she wasn't really able to do anything academic. Her confidence had been totally undermined.

She never told me anything about sex at all. It was never, never mentioned. The only thing my mother did for me was when I was 12 or 13. I opened the drawer in my bedroom and here was this belt and pins and these awful pads made out of barber towels. I didn't know what they were for – my mother had sneaked them in for me to find and I wouldn't dare ask her. I only had a vague idea. I don't know who first mentioned periods to me. Certainly we had no instruction on hygiene at school.

I met my husband during the Second World War. Groups of girls from work used to go to dances and I met him at one of those. I was always the wallflower, nobody ever came and asked me to dance – I don't know why I went, it was terrible. So when he came and asked me to dance I was grateful, I suppose. My parents didn't like him. My father thought he was awful, and so he was, because he was on sick leave all the time. He used to have a walking stick, pretending he was lame, and he wasn't at all. He'd injured his foot in a motorcycle accident a number of years before and his foot was misshapen but he'd limp across the parade ground to go to sick parade. Mum never ever said very much but I know she didn't like him. I was close to her but I think as you get to be a teenager you are inclined to leave your mother and your family behind. I thought I knew it all – don't we all?

I was 19 when I got married. I was pregnant and Mum was distressed about that. We had a wedding in the garden at home. I really loved home and we had quite a few people there, but it was an awful day. I can remember saying to myself, 'I shouldn't be doing this', but there wasn't any alternative in those days. And Frank's people were very good to me.

We had no money, nowhere to go, nothing. We rented the front half of a house, it was freezing cold and there were no facilities. To get to the laundry I had to go out the front door and right round the house. Our first child, a son, was born there. My mother loved my baby, she was always knitting, she wrote a lot, and she and Dad used to come down quite often. They had a car, but money was scarce – you didn't just hop in the car and whiz down for a Sunday afternoon visit. Oh, it was dreadful there.

Then we moved to a proper state house in another town, so that was a bit of an advance. My parents were closer and by that time I was pregnant again. Frank used to go out a lot and leave me by myself – it was very lonely. He was very brutal and cruel, but his parents made up for a lot because they'd come in and bring me eggs and things from the farm.

I had my second child at home by myself, without the doctor. I didn't know anything about the signs and pains coming so many minutes apart. So I had him in the night and then Frank had to rush away to try and find a doctor. I didn't even know about the cord. The doctor said, 'Is there something I could have to tie the cord with?' so I had to tell them where to find the crochet cotton. Mum couldn't help – I don't think she knew much herself. I would never have fed the baby in front of anybody: you didn't have breasts or anything, they were just non-existent; you didn't even go to the toilet if you were within earshot of anybody, they might hear you passing water. We had a very straight-laced home like that.

I struggled on. It was terrible with no money and Frank out of work half the time, bashing me up. I had rheumatic heart disease because as a child I had had rheumatic fever and by my late teens I was noticing some restriction in my activity. So having the children, I was exhausted. I had no washing machine – I had to wash dozens of nappies and sheets and wring them out by hand. The weather was so cold, the sun never shone and the washing never got dry. Frank would often stay away overnight. I couldn't leave – there was nowhere to go, no money, and if you left, you left with what you stood up in. You couldn't take a thing from the family home. You were just a chattel compared to now.

When my second child was eight I got pregnant with Jane. When I was pregnant I got more and more tired. I'm absolutely amazed at the girls now who can go to work to their eighth month – I used to have to go and sleep all the time. I wasn't coping and my husband used to get wild and knock me down because I was too tired to do anything. He was a very bad sport, very quick-tempered, so family activities were always spoilt.

I had really wanted a daughter for many years. We lived next door to some people who had a little girl, Colleen, and I wanted a little girl like Colleen. I must have gone on about it quite lot, so Frank said, 'If you want a daughter, you're going to get one', and it turned out I did, so that was wonderful. I can remember being in the home. I was up in the second storey and my eldest boy was there with one set of grandparents – they wouldn't let children in to visit in those days – and he was calling out to me, 'What do you want for your birthday, Mum?' I said, 'Oh, I've got all that I want, dear. I don't want anything else.'

So I got my girl and she was the light of my life but I still did a lot for the boys. They had ponies and I used to be secretary of the Pony Club and I watched their football and swimming. They weren't left out of it, but they were at school by then. Of course my mother used to come just about every day to see this beautiful creature. And her father loved her too – doted on her. She was very special for me and couldn't do anything wrong.

I suffered on behalf of the children. Even if I could have gone I don't know that I would have, because I thought it would be worse with the two boys and Jane, trying to make it on my own. You didn't get any money and I thought I'd be going from the frying pan to the fire. I used to clear out overnight because Frank would attack me – I'd run up the road to a friend or neighbour's and come back in the morning. My mother was too gentle to intervene. She would do little helpful things like coming down and doing the ironing – that was her way of making it a little bit better for me, minding the children sometimes, bringing me a present, comforting things. But there was no way she could tackle Frank because she'd never encountered anybody who went into rages.

JANE: Being a daughter to my mother was good, but being a child in the house was terrible. It was just awful. And it was never talked about – bad marriages, wife beating, it was never discussed. Either people didn't know or they knew and didn't know what to do. And if they did know, there was nobody to go to anyway. Nobody took a stand on Mum's behalf, and yet there were family who should have helped. When there's a violent man around, other people are afraid, not just the wife. The men stomp round saying, 'She stays so she must like it.' Nothing is further from the truth. Who would like being beaten up? Honestly, you live in a state of terror. And nobody even said to me, 'Are you all right?' A simple question like that would have meant so much.

From when I was really tiny, I was always my Dad's favourite – I was 'Lollipop'. I can remember just loving that. I couldn't wait for Dad to come home. I really loved my Dad. I think I can remember when I realised that things were not right, but sometimes the memories and the reality are different. I remember one day helping my mother with the baking, which I loved to do. She'd made a loaf or something, she put it in the oven then whipped it out, saying, 'Oh I haven't put the sugar in' – the sugar was still in the cup on the bench. So she stirred it all in the cake tin and said to me, 'Oh, that's what happens with you talking to me all the time.' Well, I thought, I'm not having this, so I got down off the stool – I was about four – and I went outside to my father and burst into tears. I did it on purpose and he said, 'What's the matter?' 'Mummy growled at me because she said I made her forget the sugar.' Well, he came in and shouted and bashed her up. The penny dropped at that point when I realised that my mother didn't do anything to deserve that kind of response. So I became Mum's ally instead of Dad's favourite.

We used to wait with bated breath for him to go away and then heave a huge sigh of relief because he was gone for a week. I used to spend a lot of time planning to murder him and I never did actually work out how I was going to kill him and not get caught. I didn't want to go to jail – I didn't want to leave my mother. Mind you, I used to think about suicide a lot, too, but I always worried about leaving Mum by herself to cope with Dad.

As a teenager I was a real mess. I was very much a loner at school because my life was so different from everybody else's. They all had Mums and Dads and proper families who all did things together and got on and the girls liked their fathers. I used to think that they were lying. When Dad was there we were never allowed to laugh because it made too much noise. We weren't allowed to eat apples or toast, because he couldn't stand the crunching.

We used to wait in absolute terror if he was home and he'd gone out to the club. You knew what was going to happen – lying awake in bed waiting for all the bumps and the thumps and shouting and not knowing what to do and being physically too small to do anything. And too young. I did call the police more than once but they were no help. Mind you, they did scare the hell out of Dad – he was just a coward and would only hit people who couldn't hit back.

It was just dreadful, and when I was married my husband's family used to argue a lot too. One time Phil and I were in the spare room and his parents were arguing in the bedroom and I just shook like a jelly. I hadn't been like that for years and it all just came back.

PEGGY: When Jane was 14, Frank was so wild he got all my clothes and threw everything out the front door. I was just about cheering, because if I got thrown out I had some legal property rights. So that was absolutely marvellous. I said, 'Come on, get all this stuff into the car.' My mother didn't live very far away and we went up there. The boys had left home by then and my father had passed away before that, so when we went and lived with Mum it was just the three generations of women living together and we had lovely times.

I used to do some typing for a public typist when the children were babies but as Jane got older I worked for a real estate agent part-time. Then when the marriage had gone and I was definitely not going back, I got a more permanent job because I had to have money. Eventually I got a job at the hospital – I'd had a heart operation and decided I'd like to be a medical typist. At the marriage settlement I said I didn't want any maintenance for Jane but I wanted the house, so the house was signed over to me and I continued to pay the mortgage and maintain Jane.

It was wonderful when we moved back into our family home, but he had wrecked it. There were tacks and old food and cocoa powder all over the carpet in the lounge; he'd set fire to the curtains, and the venetian blinds were all broken. The wallpaper and wallboard was all scoured with a nail or something, and there was broken glass and bottles all emptied out in the laundry. We had to start from scratch and fix it up.

Jane stayed at home until she finished secondary school then went down to the CIT (Central Institute of Technology) at Petone. That was a bit of a failure. I wanted her to do something – I don't know whether I was wrong in influencing her or not. I wanted her to be a physiotherapist or an occupational therapist, I thought she was that smart.

JANE: I was really quite keen to go to CIT because I'm good at needlecraft, handcrafts and that kind of thing. It was a combination of that and wanting to care for people and do my bit, I suppose. I did a year there, but at school I never did a lick of homework or anything – just cruised on through, never tried, never worked hard. I didn't know what the hell had struck me at CIT – I mean you had to do all this work at home! Shock, horror! It just didn't dawn on me that what you did in tutorials and lectures and everything wasn't it – you had to do hours and hours and hours of it at home.

I had the ability, just didn't have the drive. You don't when you're a teenager. You have no idea of what you want to do. I thought all my school life that I was a science person – I was always in the top stream of everything – but when it really came down to it there was no way I could understand physics, it was like a foreign language to me. I'm an arts person. So I was doing wrong things, aiming in the wrong direction as well.

I started off in a hostel and that was pretty awful so we all moved out and got into a flat. We had a wonderful time. That was the beginning of the end, because I actually had a part-time job as well as a hectic social life. Then I met Phil and that was the end of that.

I knew it was a very difficult relationship, but I kept on thinking, 'Well, he's not my father and I'm not my mother, it's not the same, we're different people – it won't be the same', but basically it was. You're 17 and the world's at your feet, you know it all. I thought, 'No, the relationship won't be the same and I'll make it work.' I used to say that to myself I don't know how many times – 'I'll make it work.' I lived with Phil for about two years, until I turned 20. We got married at his family home and I remember thinking, 'I shouldn't be doing this.' But I'd lived with him already and I thought it was too late to change anything.

PEGGY: I hated it – I wouldn't go to the wedding. It turned her mind. So there were a few years there where we were different people. It was awful, the division and the strain. Nobody got on – oh God, it was horrible. I could see that Phil was useless. I thought, 'What's Jane letting herself in for? Can't she see that she'll be keeping him all her life?' He had a type of muscular dystrophy.

In the intervening time my mother passed away. It was not as difficult as it might have been in some respects because my mother was a very independent person – loved her garden and kept her house so lovely and because she was getting older she always made sure that everything was tidy. She died very unexpectedly overnight. The shock was immense, but then as I had time to think about it I thought, well if Mum had been asked that night if she would like to die tonight or have a stroke and stay on for a few years and be disabled or something, I know what she would have chosen.

She was about 72. I still miss her terribly. She comes to see me in the night sometimes.

I'm very like her in many ways because I like housework and gardening and things. She was fonder of animals than I am. Because she didn't have any education, she wasn't developed artistically or anything like that, but she did very well and kept herself modern and interested and she was always very popular. People liked my mother. She was very good – a simple not a complex personality, very even-tempered and very good to my father. She loved him. My Mum and Dad never quarrelled. The worst thing about my mother was that she would get the 'no speaks' and I learned that from her. I used to get the 'no speaks' too, and I had to overcome that.

When Jane married, she was down at Paraparaumu and I was alone in Hamilton. I'd moved out of the family state house and bought a Lockwood which I'd always wanted and I felt I was quite wealthy by this time! I was earning quite good money. So I drove down to Wellington a couple of times to see Jane. That was a disaster because I was heartbroken to see Jane going round in rags. I'd set so much store by Jane and thought she was much more intelligent than that. How could she get herself into such a state?

There was a time when we lost contact because Phil and I had a huge row. I got a stinking letter from Jane and I didn't even read it – I haven't read it to this day. I got rid of it because it started off telling me how mean I was and everything, and I thought, 'Oh this is just too awful.' I was disappointed and disgusted. I used to comfort myself by saying, 'As long as they don't have children there's always some hope.' Then she rang to say she was expecting and broken up about it. She didn't want to be pregnant and hadn't expected that she'd ever be able to because of Phil's condition. I offered to pay her fare to Australia, because that's where you had to go for an abortion. 'Oh,' she said, 'good grief.' It was a real moral dilemma for her and she decided to go ahead and have the child. That was a trial, too, because she was in labour for so long, it seemed to go on and on.

JANE: David was a very big baby, and I couldn't have him naturally, so they took me down to Wellington. At three o'clock in the morning we all hurtled down in the ambulance, and they finally did a caesarian the next afternoon.

PEGGY: Phil rang to say that she was going to have a caesar, and I had about 20 minutes to catch the plane. I couldn't believe my eyes when I saw Jane. She was like a balloon. They'd left her far too long. I saw her before she went into theatre, and Phil and I were there to see the baby. I stayed overnight then came back down a couple of days after she came home, but I got in the way all the time. Phil resented me being there.

JANE: I was so frightened. I didn't know what to do with the baby. I think he was still in a singlet and nappies, because I was too scared to put his nightie on him or anything like that. Mum was absolutely horrified that I didn't know what to do with this child and that there was no bonding with the baby.

PEGGY: We kept in touch but were not very close. David was three when Jane rang me and said, 'Can you come and get me? I'm leaving Phil.' I said, 'Yes.' So I drove down. She was in such a state she didn't know what to take and what to leave.

JANE: I left everything. The problem was that I'd been to see a solicitor and said, 'I think I'm ready to leave my husband and I don't know what to do and what I can take.' He said, 'You can take nothing, it's all matrimonial property, you're not entitled to anything', and I thought, 'Oh well, I suppose that's the law', so I said, 'What about all the stuff I had before I got married?' No, I couldn't take that either. So I left it all and I walked out. I wouldn't do that now, though. We women need to realise that we can fight! The law is not necessarily justice and it can be manipulated. I should have taken everything I wanted and given it back if I had to. It is not easy to rebuild your life, beginning from a potato peeler upwards.

PEGGY: She came back to live with me, but David was such a handful. Jane and I had a great relationship but we were jointly concerned about David. I felt equally responsible. I thought he'd get better when he was in a nice quiet environment, but he didn't really.

He was a hard kid to manage. Jane and David were with me for about nine months, then she got a little one-bedroom flat nearby. Jane was working and David was going to daycare – I would often go and pick him up. Then she bought a section and built a house. As the years went on I used to say to Jane, 'You know, we should be living in one house. It would be nice if we could live together.' But really it was David who was the problem.

JANE: I thought, 'How could Mum stand this child if we were all in one house? I can't cope – how on earth is she going to put up with it?' I had a job as a sales rep and was away every second week for the week. I'd had years of having live-in housekeepers and child-minders. The last one I had was just wonderful with David, but I'd come home on a Friday absolutely exhausted and there'd be a week's worth of washing lying in the laundry and dishes in the sink. And all they'd eaten was spaghetti and bread and milk all week. I was at the end of my tether, I was so tired. I had a girl for the best part of a year and when she left at the end of the university year I couldn't get anybody. I even had an ad on the radio. But all the fruitcakes come out of the woodwork if you put an ad in the paper for a live-in housekeeper!

Then Mum said she'd have a go. She was retiring from work at that stage and said maybe David could come and stay with her when I was away. Things fell into place, but not marvellously because he was pretty tough on her. Before that I had a whole system set up where there was me first, then the housekeeper or the daycare centre and then as a backup in an emergency there was Mum. If all else failed there was always Mum, but the initial pressure wasn't on her. With only her, there was no failsafe mechanism at all. Then she got sick and went to hospital and it was the end of the world, really. It was just awful.

Repping's not an easy job. People think you just cruise around, stay in motels and drive in big cars, but it is hard work a lot of the time and it's difficult to run a house and have a child, not to mention a difficult child as well. It was always such a battle to keep going and do well at the job. But I didn't want to do any other job. I've been repping for eight years now and I have never enjoyed anything like this in my life. I love it, absolutely love it. I've had more fun working the last eight years than I've had in my entire life. The work's good, the product's good, the customers are good.

PEGGY: After six years David was becoming older and more impossible. He and Jane were coming to physical violence and we couldn't get any help from anyone.

JANE: We ended up at Parentline after I'd tried to get help from all sorts of other places – it was the end of the line. Mum had been in hospital and I'd been dashing in and out to her and dashing around after David, and as soon as everything came right I fell down in a big heap. So I got sick too. I remember saying to a girlfriend, 'I don't know what I'm going to do. The only thing I can think of to get any help with David is to drive under a truck.' She got so worried about me that she started ringing round and put me on to Parentline. They were marvellous but their hands are tied – they're only a voluntary organisation. They had the brilliant idea that we get involved with the Social Welfare in the hope that I could get some assistance with David.

Social Welfare decided to have a family group conference and it was decided that boarding school would probably be the best idea, but I couldn't afford it on my own. That group conference ended up as a huge farce. It was just a big joke. You couldn't believe that these highly educated and trained people who were supposed to know what they were doing could end up in such a ridiculous situation. It was absolutely ghastly. The result of this traumatic meeting was zero: Phil and his family wouldn't help, Social Welfare wouldn't help. Nothing!

The very worst of it is that you carry all this emotional baggage around with you. There's times when you think you've got rid of it all, or you've accepted it and come to terms with things. But when I was having the hassles with David with Parentline they wanted him to go to counselling and they wanted me to go to counselling as well, so I did, but they dredge it all back up. They don't just go through your own bad marriage, they go through your parents' marriage. They never actually tell you how to fix things. That's the annoying thing. You can work out what's wrong yourself, but when you're in the problem you don't know how to fix it, you don't know how to change what's already there and they don't tell you that either. It only makes things worse because it makes you feel even more inadequate as a parent.

It really came home to me after the Social Welfare meeting that nobody was going to help. It didn't matter who I went to or what I did, there was nothing. David was 11 by that stage and I felt quite honestly that within five or six years one of us would be dead and it was probably going to be me. I just didn't know what to do. I cried on and off for about three weeks. I said to Mum, 'I can't go anywhere else, there's nowhere left to turn. I'll sell the house and he will have to go to boarding school.' So that's what I did. Mum said, 'What are you going to do?' I said, 'I'll go flatting again, I've done it all before, more than once, I can do it all again.'

PEGGY: I said, 'Well, if you sell your house, I'll sell mine.' We managed to get David into boarding school and we put both our places on the market. I reckoned mine would sell first but it didn't – Jane's sold and she had to move out of her place. So they moved in with me. It was a bit of a crush in the unit.

I'd been looking at houses and this was the fourth place we'd looked at. I knew we'd like it, I knew Jane would like it, and we came back together that evening and took it straight away. The arrangement was that I would buy the property and Jane would pay the bills.

JANE: I had the income and Mum didn't, but she had the capital whereas I needed my capital for the school.

PEGGY: So that's what we've done for a year now and I keep saying to Jane, 'Are you sure you can afford all this power and everything?', but she says, 'Yes, yes.' I've lived in such an economical fashion since babyhood – we had to when I was little because there was the Depression. But it's been really easy to adjust.

JANE: I notice the change a little bit because I have some fairly unusual people as friends – people who used to turn up at 11.30 at night for a bed or a meal or whatever. That's finished. They don't do it now. I also used the stress as a motivation thing, both for work and at home, and now there is no stress. I have had to find other challenges to motivate me.

PEGGY: We have very little social life. Jane's away every second week, so you can't have much of a social life when you're not in the same town all the time. And I never had a very social life anyway. I go to golf and I'm still doing medical typing at home – that occupies a good part of my week – and the rest I spend in the garden and doing the housework and the washing and ironing. I do all those domestic things.

JANE: The pressure's gone now because I haven't got David all the time. I don't do a lick of housework any more – it's really taken some getting used to. There is such a relief of pressure for me and it's lovely to come home to a beautiful home where the surroundings are nice and everything's clean and tidy and somebody loves it. And loves you coming home and loves you being there – I love coming home.

The best thing for me is the positive support. There's always somebody who's saying you've done well, this is good or that's good. There's never anybody saying all the negative things that are wrong with you all the time. And I laugh – my God, I've never laughed so much in all my life.

PEGGY: The moral support of being together is great. The company, the fun, the sharing. If I have to make decisions I don't have to make them on my own but I know that whatever I like, Jane will like, so that makes it easy. Or if I'm in a real fix and I don't know what to do, Jane says this and this and I say, 'Yes of course, that's right.' And if I want to go and do something she'll say, 'Good on you, go for it.' That's great. There's no competition between us or anything like that – it is very supportive, a very peaceful relationship.

And we can talk about most things, although sexual things are something I can't talk about. Jane can talk to other people but I don't want to hear. But she always comes home with interesting little anecdotes of the people she's met and the things that she's done and I always look forward to her coming home. We're apart enough not to get stale.

Then there's the shared responsibility for David. He's at boarding school but he comes home nearly every weekend and I'm always here either to get him or take him back if Jane has to go away. All those things. Like the school rings up and says they've run out of name tags – I just drop them in. Lots of little things like that are helpful.

JANE: We do lots of things together. Mum doesn't like eating out or anything like that – thinks it's a tremendous waste of money! We've eaten out a few times and it's been all right but she's still not very comfortable with it so we pass on that one now. But we do things like going to the plant nursery. There's a café out there and they do lovely cappuccinos and natural food and that sort of thing, so we'll beetle off out there for a couple of hours and shout ourselves a cappuccino.

We don't envisage things changing, but life's full of surprises. I don't know what's going to happen in the future. I often think to myself I don't know what I'm going to do when Mum goes – God, I'll never survive that.

PEGGY: I'll be 67 this month but I've had two heart operations – I've got an artificial valve and a pacemaker and a bypass. I haven't got a lot of stamina going for me but I can do an amazing amount. I'll be round for a while.

JANE: My life's been different from Mum's in that I've always had a lot more choices. I've been better educated and that's a self-esteem thing as well, because Mum has always felt she's a bit dumb – she says, 'Oh, you know I'm not that clever.' But she is, she really is. It's just that she hasn't been taught and the opportunities haven't been there because the pressure to educate girls wasn't the same. I can make a lot more of my own decisions about my life. I always have been able to, whereas women of her generation weren't allowed to. It's just a whole range of things, the choice of jobs – what you want to do you can. And there have been changes in the social system, like the Domestic Purposes Benefit. Having some government support, you don't have to stay because you've got no other choice. There was nowhere for Mum to go. There was no financial support. That's been a wonderful thing.

Even when I was first married, it was very rare that a mother worked, particularly with small children. Once they got to high school she was allowed to work part-time but there weren't really any working mothers. A girlfriend of mine was pregnant at the same time as me and she said she was going back to work. I was absolutely horrified, but then, of course, come my turn, I was back at work when David was six weeks old. I took him with me to the office – that didn't work out – but I was still back at work part-time when he was about six months old and full-time when he was two. And there's been changes in the support for working women during that time. At first there was only daycare open to a set time and you paid a penalty for being late to pick your child up. We went from that to having an after-school care programme that caters for mums who might not finish work until six o'clock at night. That's a big change but it's still not very wonderful. It's not easy for the children either.

I have been lucky. All my life my mother has been there for me, even when she is doubtful about what I want to do. She has been the single most influential thing in my life. I don't know if the psychologists would say that us living together is very healthy or not, but it sure is fun. We frequently suffer from uncontrollable mirth.

Although I've had some hard times and some very unhappy times, Mum has had a lot worse. The peace in her life now has been hard won and so has the emotional and financial independence. Our lives together are precious and to be treasured. Although it's been hard, there's no way I'd give up what I've got for anybody. I've worked too damn hard for that.

PEGGY: You can't give up that independence once you get it, not ever.

Antonia

In recent years, Antonia's relationship with her mother has not been easy. The book tells her side of the story only. And that's a pity, because for years she and her mother had a close relationship. They talked, shared ideas, wrote letters and were good friends. The friendship lasted through Antonia's moves around the country and overseas, and included several visits home with a woman friend.

It wasn't until Antonia specifically wrote to tell her parents that she was a lesbian that everything changed – although nothing had changed. She and her mother had little contact for two years, which caused Antonia great pain. Recently things have begun to change, and there are some indications that the rift may be healing. Having listened to Antonia's sadness, I share her hope that this will happen.

Antonia

I had a great deal to do with my mother as a child and not much to do with my father. We lived in rural mid-Canterbury in a very small area. My father was a farm worker and my mother met him when she went there to teach.

I always talked a lot to Mum and she used to read to us – we read a lot because there weren't people near us to mix with. I used to read books about what girls do together – I didn't have any girls to do things with and I thought I was missing out. I remember talking to Mum about that. I had two sisters but they were quite close to each other, and a brother who didn't seem close to anybody then, although he is now.

My youngest sister was born when I was 13 and that was probably the first time I had a problem with my mother because I was absolutely appalled that she was going to have a child. I didn't find out from Mum and Dad – a boy said to me at school, 'Your mother's going to have a baby', and I said, 'Don't say such a dreadful thing.' I was horrified at the thought that my parents would be doing things that would lead to having children. It must have been dreadful for my mother because I wouldn't talk about it, even when I found out it was true. I wouldn't acknowledge that she was having my sister. I ignored her whole pregnancy and I was going to have nothing to do with the baby when it was born, although she's probably the one I'm closest to now.

Mum wanted us to do well at school, of course. And I wanted to do well too. I always wanted to please people – my teachers and my mother. When I went to high school I went from a class of two to a class of 30 which was a shock. When we chose our courses I did what was called Professional Non-Languages. I think Mum thought doing a language would be too much for me, and only later I thought, 'Now why didn't I do a language?' She'd grown up on a farm herself and had boarded privately when she was at school and found that hard, so I think she anticipated it being hard for me.

We moved to town when I was in the sixth form. I had thought that I'd like to go to university but I wasn't very sure and I don't think my parents would have been keen on the idea, mainly because of the cost. So I applied to go homecraft teaching and got accepted. Ghastly thought! But I think I was partly attracted to the idea because my mother had trained as a teacher and lived at a women's hostel, and I thought if I did something like teaching I'd live in one of those places too. But I don't think I was realistic about what being a homecraft teacher would be like, and I decided in the end I didn't want to do that.

I'd had a weekend job at Crothalls, at the hospital near where we lived, and I saw nurses there. I hadn't thought about being a nurse in the past, except when I was very young, but I kept on thinking about it and decided to apply. Mum was pleased when I was accepted. I possibly did talk about jobs with her but I can't remember her saying I should be one thing or the other – she just wanted me to train in something. She'd have been pleased if I'd been a teacher too. In fact, I ended up being a nursing tutor for 10 years.

I lived in the nurses' home to start with, then went flatting with a friend, but that was a disaster and I went home again for about six months. That was quite hard because I'd been away and everybody else was still at home. We only had a three-bedroomed house. We had a sleepout but it was still quite cramped, so me coming back wasn't great. I went flatting again and never lived at home again after that, although I used to go home on my days off. That was a good time because Mum and I did lots of things together – my youngest sister was still at home so Mum was at home too. I enjoyed that. We talked a lot together.

I spent a year as a staff nurse then went to a hospital in another area. I thought then that I was heterosexual and I wanted to be like my other friends who were all getting engaged and married, so one of the reasons I went was that I had met a chap whom I quite liked. But I think I wanted to get away from where I trained, too. Even then I still went home quite frequently for weekends and days off, so I still had contact with Mum. I suppose I wrote, too. I remember my mother telling me that she used to write to her mother once a week. I don't think I managed that!

After two years I applied for and got a tutor's position in another hospital board area, and they sent me to Wellington for a year to do my Diploma of Nursing. That was a really, really good year. I was 23 and that was the year I realised I was a lesbian. When I was in my first job after finishing my training I remember people talking about some lesbians and being quite derogatory about them. I never made any connection between having only women friends and being lesbian because I didn't see it in those terms. I was still thinking that I would be attracted to men, although I knew I wasn't, or I never ever did anything about it so I presumed I wasn't. At that stage it was really hard to find books on lesbians. It wasn't something you could read about.

I became very friendly with another nurse and for the first two terms we did everything together – we went to the movies together, we ate together. Then she decided that we were having too much contact and should mix with all the others. I remember being absolutely devastated. I tried to talk to her because it suddenly dawned on me what I felt for her but she wouldn't talk to me about it. I was outside her door at her hostel, trying to talk to her, and she wouldn't open it and I thought, 'Oh dear, how am I going to cope with this?'

My parents came up for a weekend when I was in the middle of that. Mum had no idea until about four years ago what was going on. We never ever talked about relationships in that way, although she knew I had lots of women friends and no men friends.

I had my first relationship when I went back to my tutor's position about a year later. I met another nurse and lived with her for two years. We both knew that what we had wasn't going to last because it was the first relationship like that for both of us. I also knew it was something that would be disapproved of and that's why it was hidden.

At one stage I was told that if I was a lesbian, being a nursing tutor wouldn't be the right sort of job for me to be in. I think it was the worry that I might want to be involved with the students. At that stage I didn't really think I was a lesbian. I was just a feminist, which of course was quite radical then. A good friend who didn't even know that I was thinking these things fixed me up with a chap and I sailed into the Graduation Ball with him to try and look as though I wasn't a lesbian! It was a really stressful time. I had a car and one morning I got up and somebody had written 'lesbian' in yellow crayon over it which was really hard to get off and I got things through the internal mail about lesbians, so obviously it was seen as being an issue. It was a really hard time.

Then I met the person I lived with for 13 years. We lived in that town for about a year then moved. We said we were never going to be hidden again, because it was just so stressful. You're always worrying that somebody is going to find out. I used to imagine that somebody would throw a brick through the window and take a photo to use as evidence!

When we were moving we stopped off at my parents' place. We slept in a caravan outside because there wasn't enough room inside for us. We weren't demonstrative to each other in front of my parents but they knew we were good friends. They knew we owned a car together, but it was never talked about. One night my brother was watching a TV programme about homosexuality and he said, 'Oh they're talking about gays – are you gay?' and nobody said a word. Everybody was staring fixedly at the TV and it just passed. I wasn't sure if my parents heard or even comprehended what he meant.

Our family has never been demonstrative – my parents and I have never been the sort of people who touched each other. My partner said to me, 'Your family are very undemonstrative. You have to make the move yourself and this is a good chance to be demonstrative with your parents.' I remember it was dreadful because we had to leave early. Mum and Dad were waiting to say goodbye and I lunged forward and hugged my mother, which was all right, although she was probably startled. Then my father hugged me – I think I knew that if I was hugging my mother, I had to hug my father as well. Then we hopped in the car and drove off. I was crying because it seemed like the end of one thing and the beginning of something else, and in a sense it was, because we were coming to the city to lead a new and different life.

Mum and Dad stayed with us in our new home. I had told my sisters I was lesbian – they all knew a long time before my parents. In fact my younger sister lived with us for 18 months. But when my parents came and stayed we changed everything round so that they slept in our bed and we moved into the spare room and slept in the two single beds.

Lots of times I would have liked to talk to my mother but I knew I couldn't because I didn't think she and Dad would approve because of their religious beliefs. I just knew they wouldn't. My partner had told her parents before they met me and that was a horrendous experience because they didn't really accept it. The thing that worried me was that everybody else except my parents knew at that stage.

After we moved I finished a BA I had been doing extramurally, then did Honours. My parents came to visit again when I graduated and stayed with us. I always thought they must have known but Mum said later that she didn't. I thought they must have guessed because my partner and I did everything together – we went on holiday together, in fact the first nine years we lived together we didn't have a night apart. When I visited my parents, my partner was there as well, so although I still talked to Mum a lot, she was there when we were talking.

Later we went overseas for two years and towards the end of that time my father had a heart attack and I came home. My three sisters were all there and it was really interesting because the three of us spent all this time talking with my mother, and even though we were there because my father was ill, I really enjoyed it because of the talking. But I still didn't say anything. Our family never did talk about those really, really personal things.

I went back overseas and thought quite a bit about telling Mum and Dad, because I felt being a lesbian was a big part of me and they didn't know. I found it really hard, so I came back to New Zealand without telling them and worked for a year nursing. I was also thinking about doing a Masters degree but ended up starting a PhD. I knew I wanted to do something about women – I was looking at women in the ministry and I spent a year thinking about that before I decided I really wanted to do it on lesbians and religion. I thought, 'Well if I do that, I've got to tell my parents.'

My parents came up for Christmas and we all had Christmas dinner together. My partner was there as well and I always remember Dad saying grace and saying, 'Thank you that she can share it.' I thought, 'Oh dear.' After Christmas I wrote to my parents because I knew I wouldn't be able to go to their place again without telling them. I wrote two letters – a separate letter to Mum and one letter to Mum and Dad – which was interesting in itself because I felt I wanted to tell Mum more than I told Dad. I remember posting the letter and thinking, 'I can't get it out now, it's in the box, it's going, I can't get it back.' If I could have I would have sawn open that box and retrieved it.

I didn't hear anything for ages. Well, it seemed ages, but I suppose it was only about a week and a half or two weeks. Mum wrote back – Dad never wrote, ever – and said it was a complete shock because she had never ever thought about it, it had never once crossed her mind, she thought that my partner and I were good friends. But I'd written to her and I was still her daughter, her eldest daughter, so I was special in that sense and she would need time to get used to it. I felt really positive about that letter. I thought, 'Oh, that's good', because it wasn't what I expected. I felt really relieved. When I'd written I said to Mum that if she wanted to talk to the minister I was quite happy for her to do that because I didn't know who she would have to talk to, but I said my sisters and brother knew.

Anyway, I got another letter about three weeks later. Mum wrote for her and Dad, and said that they'd thought about it and in view of their beliefs they couldn't accept it because they thought it was wrong. They could accept it if we weren't living together, but as long as I was living in a relationship then they couldn't come here and we couldn't go there together. That was a great shock. I kept trying to write for a while and then I stopped. Finally I wrote a letter saying that I wasn't going to write any more because I found it too difficult. I was denying a part of what I was and I was denying my partner if I pretended that she didn't exist and I couldn't do that. I didn't have any direct contact with my parents at all for two years. It was dreadful.

I used to hear about them from my brother and sisters so I knew what was happening. They moved houses in that time, and I heard bits about what they thought. Mum talked to my sister who lived near them and I was pleased that she did, but I don't think Dad ever talked about it at all with anybody.

About two years later, things changed by chance. We were in the same city as my parents, on holiday, and our car broke down. I hadn't planned on seeing Mum, although she knew that I was coming through because we stayed with my sister. My partner had a cold and was in bed so I decided to go and see Mum and Dad at their new house – and they weren't home. It was dreadful, I was all keyed up. But I decided, 'I've started this so I've got to keep doing it', so I went back again in the afternoon and they were home. It was strange because I was really nervous. Mum and Dad have a stained-glass cross that hangs in the door and I had these visions of my father chasing me down the road with this in his hand. Of course he didn't – they were pleased to see me. But we never talked about my relationship. It was as though those two years hadn't happened and I couldn't talk about it, I couldn't say, 'Well, here I am.' I stayed for afternoon tea and Mum said, 'Do you want to come back on Thursday?' – she'd worked out how long I was there – and I said, 'Oh yes, we'll both come', and they didn't say, 'No, you can't.' So I brought my partner with me and we had afternoon tea. I saw them once more, but we never ever talked about anything and still Mum and I didn't start writing again. I just sent things on birthdays and times like that.

I've only recently got a letter from Mum – it's the first time she's written for well over two years. We used to write regularly before then, and I found it very hard not doing that. Because she's started writing, I can respond, so I'm really pleased about that.

They did come up and visit the Christmas after that meeting. It was a strange Christmas because we were all together – that wouldn't have happened a few years before – and it was just after that that my partner said she wanted to leave. So it seemed really ironic to be there together just when the relationship was going to end. I've never actually talked to my mother about the relationship ending. In fact I've never talked to my mother alone, because Dad's always there. The one time I did see Mum briefly by herself was when Dad was at golf, but we knew he was coming home so I didn't feel I could start a big conversation – I didn't even say what had happened with my ex-partner. I just said she had decided that she wanted to leave and that I was going to stay in the house.

They actually came and stayed with me after she left. We had this huge debate about the small number of women lecturers in universities, because Dad said that if women were able to be professors then they would be. Mum was talking about the situation when she was at university and how many women staff there were, so she could see the sorts of things I was saying, although there are some things we don't agree about. It was good all of us being together. I guess I would just have liked more time. But you don't know if you'll ever get that.

I never talk about my thesis with them either and they never ask how it's going because they know what the topic is and they don't want to know what's happening. I can't ask them to my graduation for that reason, which I feel quite sad about in a way. I wonder, and this is a strange thing to say, if Dad wasn't there, whether Mum might be different. I think my parents thought that my relationship was a one-off and now I'll be okay, although when I told them I was a lesbian I said that I wasn't going to change. They have exposure to the sort of Christian groups that say you can change, or if change isn't possible, then you shouldn't do anything about it. I think they think that if I am alone then it is all right. I don't know what's going to happen now that I'm in a new relationship.

I think Mum worries – her image of lesbians is the stereotyped image that you get through the extreme right. She once said, 'She wouldn't go to bars, would she?' She had this image of what bars were. That's why I wrote her a separate letter – I tried to explain all that.

Several years ago, just after I had told my parents, I got quite depressed. I was on night duty before I came back to university, and I thought that was doing it to me – all I was doing was sleeping and going to work and sleeping and going to work. I went to a counsellor and she talked about me grieving for my mother and it being worse because she was still there. I knew what was happening, I knew how they were living their lives, but I wasn't part of it. That counselling was good – it resolved a lot of problems. I feel in control now and I don't have that anxiety that I used to have in the past.

I'm very like my mother in funny little ways. I always saw myself like her when I was growing up – she liked reading and she leads a very full life. I found it hard last year to imagine her as 70. All through her life she's been like that, she's always been involved in doing lots of things. I think in some ways we share the same values. Even though I wouldn't see myself as a Christian now, my values are very much based on that sort of ethic, and certainly lots of things I think about work and what one should do are very much based on what my mother thinks. Where we'd have differences would be on things like the family and what Mum would see as being right for the family – what sort of family she should have and raising children and that sort of thing. Interestingly enough, they've never talked with me about having children and I've never felt any pressure to marry, even before they knew about me. I think I was seen as a career person and that was okay because I did well in nursing. I think they were disappointed when I left nursing. I was doing something worthwhile and it was something they could be proud about, because they talked about it to others, whereas it's a bit hard to explain that you've got a daughter who's teaching something about religion and women and who's also doing a suspect PhD.

A postscript

When I read this account about my mother and myself, my first impression was that this is a partial picture of both of us. It doesn't show me as I am to my friends, my colleagues, to my sisters and brother; and it doesn't show my mother as she must appear to my father, her other children and her friends.

This partial view is the way it is in my relationship with my mother – by not acknowledging my lesbianism she doesn't get to see the whole me. Being a lesbian is central to my identity and it influences how I am as a partner, as a friend, as a colleague and as a teacher. It has given my life a richness that doesn't emerge in this interview and I wouldn't change the choices I have made in any way. What I would want in the future is for my mother to be able to share in these parts of my life and to be glad for me. I hope it is not too late for this to happen.

Shirley, Anne & Gill

The places we live in often shape our lives – and our relationships. In this set of three stories, Shirley and her two daughters describe what it was like growing up on an isolated farm, four hours by sea and road from the nearest city. The farm and its setting dominated their lives and to some extent affected the choices they could make, especially in regard to school and work.

If the farm provides continuity and context, it doesn't guarantee uniformity. Anne and Gill have had very different lives and different relationships with their mother. All three are creative, independent and practical. They are also very loyal, and have protected each other in discussing their difficult times and the differences between them, just as they have supported each other through their lives.

I interviewed them separately, but on one perfect day in Nelson we ate lunch together in the sun, looking out over the bay. I enjoyed their closeness and obvious delight in each other's company. It seemed a small thing to respect their privacy in return for a trio of sturdy stories and a breath of rural New Zealand.

Shirley

I had a great childhood, a wonderful childhood. What is now a built-up area was then orchards and fields going right down to the sea. We knew everyone, either well or by name. My two brothers and I had space to roam. We made aeroplanes from sycamore seeds and necklaces from barberry berries, and every spring there was a nest in an old hollow fencepost at the top of the lane next to our house. I always felt my mother was a bit ahead of her time because she allowed me so much freedom. She was keen on poetry and writing – I always admired her handwriting which was full of character and dash. My father was a great one for writing humorous verses. Both Mum and Dad were musical. My mother played the piano and my father the violin. He was a foundation member and for a time deputy-conductor of the Nelson Male Voice Choir. With that background, I suppose it was natural that I should learn both piano and singing. Mum and I played duets together. We had a very good relationship.

St Barnabas' Church, where my father was vicar's warden and a lay reader, was an important part of our lives. When the organist married and my father said he had put my name down to take her place, I wasn't too pleased. I was only 14 and the thought of being committed to two services every Sunday didn't appeal. In fact, I was organist for eight years until I married there.

They were Depression times when we were young and although it must have been difficult financially for my parents they saw to it that we all received a college education. I have always been grateful for that. Before I left college, war had been declared. One by one my elder brother and all our friends left to go to war on the other side of the world. So many didn't come back. I was in shows staged to raise money for the Patriotic Funds. We travelled round the district and further afield by bus, putting on our shows. I also worked in the canteen at the aerodrome some evenings, serving supper to the boys at the Basic Training School. I had a job as a proofreader on the *Nelson Evening Mail* and sometimes when work was finished I'd go up to the public hospital to work. I lived at home, which was the usual thing if you didn't join the Forces.

I met my husband before he went overseas. He was training to be a pilot. He declared, often enough for me to believe it, that he said to his friends, 'That's the girl I'm going to marry', before we were even introduced. Later he became a Spitfire pilot and was awarded the DFC.

We married just after he returned at the end of the war and went to live on the family farm on D'Urville Island. I went to a life far removed from the one I'd been used to, in more ways than one. Access was by sea only in those days, which made us very isolated. Our nearest neighbour was four miles over the hills by walking track. A journey to French Pass in our launch took two hours and to Nelson four hours if the sea was reasonably calm.

I came from a fruit-growing district, so life on a sheep farm was another world to me. The steep hills were a real challenge, rising from sea level to over 2,000 feet behind the woolshed. It was no place for my bicycle – every walk was a climb. I was lucky to have a supportive mother-in-law who eased me into taking over from her before she left the island. Nearly everything was new for me. I had to cook for the farm hands, bake bread every day and make butter when the cream jars were full. I learned how to cut up sheep – a sheep was killed for the house every week – and we had venison and wild pork the men brought home from hunting. In those days we had no freezer, which meant that in the summer some of the house meat went to the dogs.

If anything could have put me off living there it would have been my first visit. A launch put me ashore in a bay where I was met by my father-in-law-to-be. He was carrying a stout manuka stick. He pushed it through the handle of my suitcase, swung it over his shoulder and we trudged 1,200 feet up and four miles over the hills to the house. I was young then, and I didn't think there was anything unusual about my introduction to my future life.

I was fortunate because leisure time was never a problem for me. My piano had arrived, hoisted up on to our jetty from one of the coastal boats operating then. I enjoyed writing, painting and gardening, but I had less time for these interests later on, with three children under three, and men to cook for. I didn't miss my family and old home as much as I thought I would, but being able to be in contact by phone helped, and my mother was a regular correspondent.

I've always thought it was more of a man's life than a woman's on an isolated farm. The women who go there have to have a certain disposition. It's not like living in a community where it's easy to get from A to B and women can follow a particular bent or interest. Women who are unable to get through the day without visiting friends or the local shops would possibly find it difficult to adapt to such a life. Our nearest store was two hours away by sea, the nearest neighbour four miles over the hill by foot or horseback, and the mail and stores came once a week. We had to keep an open house and get along well with the neighbours, even when they didn't have the same interests. And it's very important for a woman on the farm to have her own interests. The children go off to boarding school when they get to college age – they can continue with Correspondence School but it's a pity if they don't learn to mix with others – and unless the woman has a close interest in the farm or interests of her own, it can be a very lonely life. However, loneliness was not one of my problems; there was no time for it. In fact I would have appreciated more leisure time.

We had a son three years after we married. Nearly two years later he was drowned in one of the creeks near the house. That painful time is like a wound scar – you can cover it up but it is always there. My support at that time was my elder brother's wife who came and stayed a while through a time that must have caused her great stress. At the end of that year I had Anne; 14 months later I had Gillian; then another son.

My parents didn't visit the farm much. Neither of them was a great sea traveller. The very thought of the four-hour sea trip by launch bothered them, especially my father. Soon after he arrived he would start worrying about the return journey. But I saw them when I went to town.

Getting medical attention was a problem on the island. The

area had no district nurse then and the doctor had to come by boat. When the babies were due my husband couldn't get rid of me quickly enough! When Anne was about nine she began complaining of severe pain in her right leg. Nothing was diagnosed until the doctors found her right leg had become thinner than her left. They sent her to Wellington Hospital for six weeks for tests. I stayed with her all that time, going backwards and forwards to the hospital. I was fortunate to have my husband's sister in the same area but on the mainland, and she looked after the two younger children while I was in Wellington. Although the children had had the polio vaccine, the doctors decided it was polio that affected the right side of her body. It still troubles her if she does more than her body can cope with.

I taught the children through the Correspondence School until they went away to boarding school. Anne went when she was 11, but boarded with friends for the first year. Gill didn't go until secondary school age. None of them liked it because they'd had the freedom of the farm, with their horses and the animals and the tennis court we'd made for ourselves. The school had rules like, 'You can't go outside that gate without permission', and of course they felt restricted.

When they left school, neither of the girls had a definite idea of what they wanted to do. Anne took a nurse/receptionist course up north. Gillian began working with an advertising agency in Wellington and then did an agricultural course at Massey University. By this time we had a small daughter by adoption. This meant that after a year or two I was once again supervising Correspondence School lessons.

The girls were good correspondents and mail day was the high spot of our week. Once a week the mail launch made a circuit of the island, bringing in stores and mail and taking away the outgoing mail. We knew that if we didn't write and send out a letter that day it would be another week before it went. Now with letters, I'm inclined to think, 'Oh well, it can go tomorrow', and in the end I don't write so much. The girls didn't ring as often as they do now. In those days we maintained our own telephone line, which often let us down in stormy weather – the line followed the shoreline and in places passed through thick native bush. We had our own generator then, too – power from the mainland came much later.

Over the years we had many interesting visitors – geologists, yachtsmen, journalists and photographers, palaeontologists, two governors-general (who arrived by helicopter), trampers and others. My husband developed Hodgkin's disease, and from that time until his death five years later he was in and out of hospital, ever hopeful, ever determined. It was this determination that towards the end of his life took us to visit a wartime flying companion – Ian Smith, at that time prime minister of Rhodesia.

The girls weren't really city girls, and I don't think they really enjoyed being away from the farm. Both of them were married by then. Anne had married very young. I wasn't happy about the marriage, mainly because of Anne's youth – scarcely out of school! The person one goes overboard for at 18 is seldom the one one would choose a few years later. And so it proved. I admire Anne for having the courage to make the break instead of letting things drag on. Faced with such a situation I doubt if I would have had such courage. Gill had met her husband at Massey. The girls have always made their own decisions and been very independent. We've always been close, but there have been some special times and sadnesses like the loss of their father and the end of Anne's marriage.

After my husband's death I decided to leave the farm in the care of Anne and Gill and their husbands. Both of them were on the farm by then. I was in the main homestead; the other house on the farm was four miles away, which meant a lot of travelling to and fro for them. With hindsight, I left too soon. I should have thought about things longer.

I moved to a flat in town with my adopted daughter. At first I worked as a nurse-aide in a private hospital from 11 at night until seven in the morning. A friend down the road lent me her bicycle to get to work. It had no lamp so I pedalled quickly along the quieter streets until I heard a car coming, when I'd hop off and walk until it passed! Then I had a letter from a friend up north who was on the board controlling three private schools. She suggested I take on the job of matron at one of them. It was a live-in position and my young daughter could be a pupil there, so I decided to go, and stayed a term short of two years. Interestingly enough, later on I was a board member of those schools for nearly six years. By then I was remarried to a local solicitor. The girls found it difficult when I remarried, although they're fine about it now. My adopted daughter was most unhappy at that time. She probably felt, mistakenly, that she was losing me. Her school achievements suffered as a result. She is now a wife and mother of three, taking an active part in her community. Our relationship is close but because of distance we don't see as much of each other as we would like.

Both Anne and Gill have three children – Anne has three boys, and Gill a girl and two boys. The children are another tie between us and it's a lovely one. It's interesting to see family characteristics, physical and otherwise, carried on in another generation. I realised that the girls were going through the same things that I had to go through – they had the same problems, the same stresses, the same happy times. But I knew from experience how fragile all that is.

I'm sure both girls have a bit of me in them – different things perhaps. Anne sometimes says, 'Oh, I can see myself getting like you, Mum.' I say, 'Well don't make it sound so dire!' Both the girls are very artistic, with quite individual ways of expressing this. Gillian has illustrated a children's book of my poems which we have published. I knew Gill would be good at that. When she was quite small she'd draw on anything, including material if there was no paper handy. Funnily enough, when she got older she didn't want that sort of career, but now she's very interested and it will be marvellous for her when the last child goes to school to have more time, although of course she has the farm as well. Anne is also artistic but in a different way. She enjoys painting and she's a great storyteller. Her sense of humour must have helped tremendously over times of indifferent health and personal unhappiness. She is resilient and sensitive. We are probably closer now than we have ever been.

I feel Gill's a stronger person than I am. Physically she's almost stoic. I don't know that that's such a good thing, but she's very strong in her beliefs, no one's going to put her down. Both of them have strengths inherited from fine grandparents and a father who was a very strong personality and a leader rather than a follower.

I would like to think my relationship with my daughters has been a positive one. We're all individuals and of course we make our own decisions. I'm sure they don't approve of all I do, any more than I approve of their every move. But they enrich my life and I'm proud of them. And I just love the warmth when my daughters come – almost the first thing when we walk up to the house is that tucking-in of the arm. We're not demonstrative people but there's that very close link there.

I like to think that they've made something of their lives. I expected to work and I expected them to work. There was enough for me to do on the farm and I couldn't have got paid work – where could I have gone for it? And Gill is a full partner in the farming of the family property. Since Anne's marriage ended and she left the farm, she's had to work to make ends meet. That's the case for a lot of women now – it's very different from our day when it was difficult to separate from your husband. Women just didn't do it, certainly not at the first sign of adversity as so often seems to be the case now. I can't think of any of my friends who left when they were younger, although one or two did later on. Women who did leave would either have had to go back to their parents or have a good enough job to be able to support themselves.

There are more pressures on women now. I think that perhaps is the main difference between the two generations. And Gill's daughter will have more pressures on her than her mother did, so I think they have to be stronger people. They have to combine so much – I don't know how some of them do it.

For all the differences, the continuities have also been important. Three of my grandchildren live in the same house I lived in and on the same site where their great-grandparents' house stood. So there is a continuity and a great bond there. When I visit I can get busy with something and feel I've never left. With the hills and the sea, the outlook doesn't change, whatever else might. We've all enjoyed the same surroundings, the same way of life, all the time learning what those who were there before us had to cope with. We have all put strengths into it and we have all drawn strengths from it. It would be comforting to think that might continue, but in this life one can never be certain of anything.

Anne

I was the second child, born 10 months after my brother was drowned. That was perhaps the most painful thing in Mum's life, and when I was born she was in deep grief. From an early age I felt a sense of remoteness in my mother; it was quite obvious to me and I always thought I was the one who was causing it. I felt that I didn't quite measure up in some way – although I don't know what I was trying to measure up to. I think I was quite a difficult child because of that. I went into myself quite a bit.

At an early age I became ill with polio. I spent a lot of time in and out of hospitals and probably drove my parents mad with worry. Living on the island we couldn't just hop down to the doctor's. So that made me feel a bit more apart. I remember both my brother and sister saying, 'Come on Annie, come and play with us', and I'd be sitting there gazing out to sea, totally in on myself. I loved the life on the island because I could dream as much as I wanted without having to worry about other people, but it was also a rather lonely feeling.

I always felt there were a lot of expectations on us as children, but as I grow older it has become clearer to me why Mum and Dad were like that – they wanted us to achieve as best we could. But at the time I rebelled against everything.

I didn't have any difficulty with the fact that I was a girl. I've always enjoyed being a female, even with all the biological problems! The growing-up years were difficult for me because I had matured physically really quickly, which was hard. But Mum was always there for me – there was always love in our household and we never went without.

I went to boarding school when I was about 11. I think that was a turning point. Mum and Dad realised that I needed the company of others my age, and although I was painfully shy it did me the world of good being sent to a school where I had to mix a lot more. I loved it and I was really quite sociable. The first year I lived with family friends. They had four daughters who were all very bright and outgoing – they didn't realise I just couldn't keep up, but it was great, I enjoyed it. Boarding school was a different kettle of fish altogether. Boarding school was a complete change of life for me and I didn't find it easy. My life was suddenly run by bells and I couldn't go at my own pace any more. Some of the rules were petty and I still remember incidents that upset and humiliated me. At that age I had shoulder-length ash-blonde hair. Coming from the island, hair dyes were unknown to me, but the matron was convinced I had dyed my hair and cut pieces off to be sent to the DSIR for testing. Another time I had to apologise to the whole boarding establishment for some minor misdemeanour. For the shy girl I was then, that was an ordeal, so I became rebellious again and my boarding school years were very up and down. My parents were always waiting for a ring to say that their daughter had been expelled!

Mum was wonderful at keeping in touch. There were always letters or phone calls. I think it must have been a very lonely time for her because the island, particularly then, was very male-orientated. We were surrounded by men – workers or stock agents, always male – and strangely enough, when I first left the island years later, one of the things that I found hardest was making female friends. Now I've got some wonderful female friends but then I was more used to the male world.

I really loved going home from school for the holidays because we were free spirits down there. There were no restrictions on us in that we could take off all day and do what we wanted to do. We had all this space – it was a wonderful childhood really. I didn't do as well at school as I could have, I spent too much time sitting at my desk dreaming. I had ability but I just didn't make the most of it. I spent my final school year at home. That was a great year in a lot of ways because I got to know my parents.

From there I went to do a course for doctors' nurse/ receptionists at Masterton Hospital. That was my introduction to flatting and that sort of thing. I enjoyed that time but I married at 18 so I wasn't on my own long. I remember I rang my parents and said that I wanted to get married – at 18 I really didn't know what I wanted. My father just said, 'Okay', but my mother went into shock and cried a lot. I was insensitive, I guess.

So I married and went to Australia for a while. We came back to the island because my father had been diagnosed as having cancer and they needed a helping hand. My husband had never been a farmer but we managed okay. We had our children there and Mum was an absolute wonder. She was just wonderful as a grandmother – she never interfered in any way, but she was always there to give a helping hand. I don't think it brought her and me any closer, though – it's only in the last few years that we've been really open and honest with one another. She was very proud of the fact that I produced three beautiful boys. She played a big part in their first few years and later on, when my marriage broke up, she had my two older sons for some years. They lived with her in Masterton and she took over the mother role.

After we'd been on the farm for quite a few years my whole world seemed to disintegrate. My father died before I had my third son. It was the first time I'd actually experienced death and to do that for the first time with someone you love dearly is shattering. I was very pregnant. I had two toddlers and life was busy – men to feed and cows to milk and a husband who really just wanted supporting himself. He couldn't see what I was going through, and of course the rest of the family were taken up with their own grief. I was still very young and everything just went completely out of my control. I sort of slid under, really. The marriage disintegrated and I wasn't capable of keeping my children together. That's one of the pains of the past, but over the years I've come to deal with it – you have to, otherwise you just go under. Now I can talk about it a wee bit. Mum took over and I say that in the nicest possible way – she was wonderful, she really was. There were no recriminations or complaints, none of that. I think it helped give a focus in her life too after Dad died.

My sister Gill and her husband were on the farm, too. Gill and I have always been close. We're completely different but we have this bond. She is the most loyal person I know. I know she shakes her head at some of the things I do, but there is still that bond. I think the marriage break-up was heart-breaking for her as well as Mum because she's a bit like Mum in a way; she'll battle on at any cost, whereas I was not prepared to do that.

I took years to recover. It's only in the last few years that I realise I've progressed. I've become more mature and now at 40 I feel I've learned a lot of lessons and I'll continue to learn a lot more. I've had a guardian angel sitting on my shoulder who's really helped me.

When I left the island I came to live in town and that was a shock. At first I was terrified. All these people seemed to be staring at me. It sounds weird, but even going to hang out the washing was difficult. I can still remember quite clearly going into town to do the shopping. I hadn't handled money much. On the island, we went into town once every two or three months. The men would write out the cheque for the food or whatever we needed and away we'd go; there was never any cash to pay out. So I had to learn all of that. I was so naive! And I was too afraid to ask for help because people would think I was silly. But that's when I started learning how to really look after myself: before that I guess I'd had quite a sheltered life.

Over those years I felt quite alone. My life and Mum's were completely different. I went through different relationships but none of them were successful and in the end she would say, 'Oh, not another one.' But that was another thing about Mum – she has never said, 'That's it, I can't be bothered with you any more.' She's always there. Of course she's been critical at times but she hasn't judged. I think my life has worried her very much, but I think she has a sneaky admiration for me too, sometimes – that I've made it, or am making it, when I might have fallen by the wayside and become an alcoholic or something. Although she would never tell me that.

I'd like to be able to sit down and talk to Mum about things that have happened in my life but in a lot of ways I don't think it would work. It might help her to understand but I think a lot of it would be quite painful for her. I know that while your mother might not agree with the things you do in your life, she has to accept them to a degree, but I would hate to think that I'd ever hurt her by telling her something. In some ways I wish I had taken the risk and talked with Mum earlier on. Our relationship might have improved more quickly. But that's how it was.

I think Mum and I are alike in a lot of ways. I would love to have known her when she was younger – she would have been fun to know. She was very attractive and had bags of go, she was very much a tomboy, a daredevil! She was very talented too and took part in concerts for the troops. So she was an interesting person and I wish she would talk more about those times. It must have been a fascinating life. She was just a young woman when she went to the island where she lived for 35 years. The first few years I think it was just her and Dad. So she went from a fairly social life to one of sheer isolation. We think it's isolated now, but the only way out then was by boat – our lives have been governed by the sea.

I never ever saw my mother idle. It was quite sad in a way, because if she ever did take a break, it was almost a guilty thing for her. It was really because of the men. I think we could have looked after her better, but our lives revolved around the men. If she wasn't looking after them she was making or creating something or gardening. Some of that still carries on with me. I still look after men – that's just the way I was brought up and I don't find it demeaning. Mum and Gill and I were not afraid to say what we thought and I felt the men respected the fact that we worked hard and were able to hold our own in their company. That's different from women I know who are completely dominated by men. Until my last breath I will fight that.

I don't know whether it comes from not having my children, but I've taken in various people over the years who have played a big part in my life – I like to help them and I get quite a bit of satisfaction from that. I don't see my children as often as I'd like now, but as they've grown older they need to live their own lives and they always say to me, 'We love you, Mum.'

I think my future's going to be better and better, and so's my relationship with Mum. I think it's wonderful that she and Gill have produced a book. As long as she can keep good health and look after herself she will go from strength to strength. She'd love to see me writing and painting too. I've always felt a slight pressure from her in that area. She'll say, 'I wish you'd do something for yourself rather than putting all that effort into other people', but I say to her, 'That has been my choice. That's what I have found satisfying.' But as I've grown older, I have felt a need to get on with something else. I just need the time.

Mum and I are comfortable together now most of the time. Sometimes I feel I would like to be able to share more of my life with her, but because a good part of my life has been painful I don't. I think that sharing will come one day, given time. But it always bothers me that I won't have the time. Something might happen to her and we won't have resolved some of the things that go back a long, long way. Mum's not a woman to sit down and have a good heart-to-heart. She wouldn't sweep things under the carpet, but she'd expect you to get on with it. Sometimes I found that really frustrating and I've just wanted to say to her, 'Slow down, stop', but I don't think she will really. I wouldn't want her any other way.

Gill

I had an idyllic childhood on the farm. I still remember saying to Mum when I reached the age of 10 that I just didn't want to grow up. I wanted to stay 10 for ever. I had an easy relationship with my mother and don't remember coming into much conflict with my parents during my teenage years.

We three children were very close in age, but as children I was probably closer to my brother than my sister because he and I shared a great interest in the outdoors. We loved to go off and explore the seashore or the hills or help Dad on the farm. Anne was more often round the house. I can still see her standing on the porch pleading with me to stay and play and me itching to be off on the farm doing something else. The time we did share was great fun because she was, and still is, a most wonderful entertainer. With her vivid imagination she would tell enthralling and often hilarious stories and these turned our pony rides into real adventures. Dad used to love having the two of us together out on the farm because Annie could really make him laugh, and with the three of us together I remember a great feeling of warmth and camaraderie.

As children we grew up with the knowledge that at secondary school level we would be going off to boarding school, but I hated the reality of it. I felt stifled and hemmed in after all the freedom and space I had grown up with, and I found the boarding hostel a cold and impersonal place. Looking back, I know that I didn't make the most of my secondary schooling. This was partly through a lack of self-confidence and maybe through a certain lack of ambition. The isolation I grew up in obviously accounts for most of this. We had very little social contact or experience of life outside the island. The only place I felt truly happy and confident was at home on the farm. Being away wasn't all painful, of course. I was an average student and parts of my schooling I enjoyed. I made some good friends and remember a lot of happy times, but I regret the large amount of time I wasted.

There were expectations on us as children to perform well, but I never felt these expectations were unreasonable for me anyway. I don't think any of us have achieved quite as highly as either of our parents would have liked, or perhaps as well as we could have. But I knew Dad wanted the farm to carry on in the family and I always felt that he thought I was just as capable of doing this as my brother. Farming was always my first love, and although I had artistic talent I never took it beyond winning the fourth form art prize. I can't remember being encouraged to do so and I didn't have enough interest in it to push it myself.

When I finished school Mum and Dad had to almost push me out of the nest because there was nowhere else I wanted to be but on the farm. It must have been so exasperating for them. Mum wanted me to do something with art, so with their help I got a job in a Wellington advertising agency. After two years I left there to enrol in a Diploma in Agriculture course at Massey University. It was fun being a student for a year and I made two lifelong friends there – my husband and the girl I roomed with. It took me a long time to mature enough to realise how much life had to offer in the wider world, and I'm very thankful that Mum and Dad had the wisdom to encourage me out into it, rather than let me cling to my safe little island home.

In between working in Wellington and studying at Massey, I spent time helping at home on the farm as Dad was ill with cancer. Mum and I got along well, though I now know that my lack of maturity prevented me from being the help and support she needed. It must have been a lonely and difficult time for her and I wasn't adult enough to help her share her fears and feelings.

After we married, my husband and I travelled overseas for eight months before coming home to farm with my sister and her husband. Dad died while we were away. It is one of my main regrets that we were all so unmindful of Mum's feelings in the period after his death. We were so caught up in our own lives, we weren't at all tuned into her grief or her needs. I kept a diary then and on the day Mum left the farm to live in Nelson, I wrote how exciting it must be for her. Looking back, I realise instead what a dreadful and lonely time it must have been.

Since having children of my own, I've come to see how much we took Mum for granted. I'm sure we were far less helpful to her than my children are to me, though she would be the first to disagree. We did have certain chores to do round the place but the brunt of work around the house and garden fell on Mum's shoulders. In the earlier years, before the advent of the freezer, she had to make both bread and butter. She spent hours toiling over a wringer washing machine, cooking on a coal range, washing up after large meals, and along with all this she had three children within three years of each other to care for. She had to teach us as well. She also had to look after a large vegetable garden and somehow found the time and energy to create beautiful flower gardens. With all that, she never lost her sense of style. We might have lived an isolated island life, but she always dressed stylishly for trips to town.

My life's much freer than hers – I have the benefit of all the mod cons electricity allows. I can spend much more time doing things I *want* to do than my mother ever could. We have better roading and transport too, so I can have much more social contact than she did. I can even to go to a meeting on the mainland. And I'm far less bound by the tradition of large farm meals. Mum nearly always had extra hands to feed as well as Dad and that meant that she had to provide a hot dinner at night and a substantial lunch. Food is still important, but it's much less dominant than it was. Of course it helps to have a microwave to thaw butter or bread at the last minute!

My relationship with my mother is very special to me. When she left the island we wrote to each other regularly, and now that she has moved closer we have almost daily phone contact. She can be tremendous fun to be with and has a mischievous sense of humour. I know she has great pride in me, both as a person and for my abilities. I often feel this pride is undeserved and that I'm unworthy of it. She has a higher opinion of me than I do and without her 'push' the two children's books we've done together would still be a dream.

It took me a long time to gain self-confidence and to be comfortable with myself. Learning to feel at ease when meeting people and in new situations is something that's grown gradually over the years. I feel a tremendous sense of freedom in finally feeling sure of myself and who I am.

My own daughter has all the confidence I never had as a child. The better roads have changed life on the island to quite an extent, so she has grown up with a far wider range of experiences and much more contact with people, especially people her own age. She went off to boarding school with a much healthier and happier attitude than I had. I think she's much more mature and perceptive than I was at her age, and I get great pleasure from her company.

I have heard other mothers say that their children wouldn't be seen walking down the street with them when they were teenagers, but I feel Georgie enjoys being with me as much as I do with her. It's easy to be anxious about her, though. There are so many dangers for growing children to face, and it's a real exercise in self-control to learn to rely on her good sense and the set of values we've already taught her. I'm glad I had the chance to bring up the children away from the constant pressure of city life – video parlours, fashion fads, violent TV and playground bullies, to name a few. And Georgie has a good relationship with Mum – they seem to have a good understanding of each other.

My relationship with Mum is very important. I am like her physically and we share several interests. I would like to be more like her in some ways – I think she has greater energy and a tremendous capacity for creative thinking. She also has a great talent as a hostess. She's warm and hospitable, she entertains with flair and people seldom leave without having their spirits lifted with laughter. She also has a sense of adventure and I'd like to think that all the things I admire her for are present in me to some extent.

There's nothing better than when we're all together as a family. It's a really good feeling. There's always lots of laughter and memories to share. It's been a good relationship, a good friendship.

Lisa & Kerry

At its best, the mother-daughter bond is a source of comfort and support. It is always there, always to be counted on. At its worst, it is destructive and endlessly disappointing. Mothers are unhappy and daughters flounder without guidance.

Lisa's relationship with her mother was at the destructive end of this continuum, while her relationship with her daughter, Kerry, has moved a long way towards the comfort end. Without a good model and a good experience to build on, Lisa had to start from scratch, coming to terms with her own life before she could be fully open to her daughter's. She is nearly there.

Kerry, still in her twenties, is younger than the other daughters in this book, but her story is an important one which tells of the shifts it is possible to make between one generation and the next.

Lisa

We've got two parts to the family – my father was married twice. I've got a half-sister who has spent most of her life overseas so I don't really know her, and an adopted sister who figured a lot in my life because she lived on a farm 30 miles away and would come in once a week. She had a family similar in age to ours and was a regular visitor at home. I didn't know until I was about 10 that she was adopted. I found out by looking through a writing desk and of course I couldn't talk about it. It really shocked me to think that nobody had bothered to say so. Someone had ripped a page out of the family history and put it in the back of the writing desk because it said that she was adopted. That's the sort of thing that happened. I went looking for things, but I could never talk about them because I wasn't supposed to see them.

Dad married Mum when he was about 50 – she was a lot younger than he was – and I was born when he was 55 and my younger sister when he was 60 years old. Dad was a solicitor. He went to work around nine in the morning and came home around eight o'clock at night. He was quite authoritarian. If he said, 'We're going out', we went out. If he said, 'Don't do it', I didn't do it. He was a reasonably fair man, although he never talked about how he felt or what he wanted. He was like a grandfather, but not an indulgent one.

I had a very unhappy childhood. Mum's mother died when she was two and she kept going back to that, but I've met people whose mothers have died when they were young and they're not like her. They don't blame everything on that or think that they can't ever cope because that happened. It's really sad, but she had lots of extended family and the children weren't left on their own.

In the space of about a minute she could turn from being a very nice woman, smiling and saying how nice everything was, to being angry and violent. I never knew whether she was going to be happy or angry or sad and I just had to react to how she was. If she was angry I got out of her road quickly – unless she caught me first. If she was sad I had to listen to all the awful things that were happening, although I was never involved with what was going on between her and Dad because he was there. She kept that separate, but she told me all about her relationships with her friends and everything else. It was bizarre. I was only about seven or eight but I listened to all her problems, and if I reacted wrongly I got beaten or thrown off into the bedroom or whatever. I didn't know what the borderline was and I could tip over it without even thinking. We often had conversations where I didn't know how they would end.

If she was angry she would be really cutting, saying things like, 'We don't have this sort of thing in our house', or 'You know very well that we never allow that sort of thing to happen and how could you possibly be thinking of it, I mean your mind must be totally dirty to think like that.' That sort of thing. She'd ask me what I was thinking. I'd say something and she'd immediately say, 'How dare you think like that? You're not allowed to think like that. You mustn't hate people and you mustn't think that kind of thing.' My mother didn't seem to have any idea that there might be another side to the story: she was right and that was that.

She could be quite violent. I remember once I had a little doll with a china face. I was sitting in a chair holding it, and she smashed it, and the only thing that she worried about was the doll. She was really sorry that the doll got smashed. She threw a shovel at me, then tipped the chair up. I don't know why she did it. That was the problem. If I'd been really bad or done something that was totally terrible, maybe; but I might have just said, 'Why?' or 'How come?' or something like that.

She was clever enough never to attack me in front of people. Once I went to stay with some family friends. I told them about Mum and the woman said to me, 'You nasty little girl, don't you ever say anything like that about your mother, ever, ever again. She isn't like that, you're making it up.' I realised then what people would say if I told them and they didn't believe me. I don't know what it's like for anybody else but I know that her attitude just made me feel I was evil and I didn't know why. When I talked to people later they'd say, 'There must have been more to it, because as a child you don't see the bigger thing', but there wasn't. When you are ironing you don't suddenly erupt and start throwing things. You're ironing, using your energy. You could say, 'I don't like what you're saying and you can get out of the room if you think you're going to talk like that', but you don't suddenly start throwing things around.

From the age of about 10 I cleaned most of the house every week. I mowed half the lawns, my sister mowed the other half and I did most of the sewing. I did all the buying of Christmas presents. The groceries were delivered so that wasn't a problem. I didn't think I did most of the running of the house but when I think back I did a tremendous amount.

Mum stayed in bed until about half-past eight or quarter to nine; she was never up when we left for school. I don't really know what she did, because till the age of seven we had a nanny in the house who worked six days a week. Although my mother never said so, the story is that she had about three miscarriages before I was born and then had a mental breakdown. She used to play the piano all hours of the night. That's what I was told, but looking back it seems that she was just a totally ineffectual person. I remember at one stage she made some curtains but it created such a hoo-haa. It took weeks, everything was all over the place and she never got it right. It was a real bind if she did something. She had money – the sewing machine was fine and the material was beautiful. She had a big allowance at the shops, she could buy anything she liked and the power bill was enormous. She had the telephone and she could drive the car – Dad would walk to work if she wanted it. There was no worry about money. I don't know what the problem was.

When I was eight I had a lot of headaches and I had trouble seeing the blackboard at school, so I asked the children beside me and got the strap on my hand for talking. It was apparently discussed with the family doctor who suggested that I be taken to the eye specialist in a nearby town. The next thing I was aware of was the doctor and my mother coming into my bedroom after I had gone to sleep, grabbing me, holding me down and forcefully putting drops in my eyes. I was held securely, feeling as though I would suffocate, and very frightened. In the morning I couldn't see properly and I couldn't go to school for several days till the visit to the specialist was organised. I was a very angry person and had many nightmares about people and things coming to get me for years after. On a positive note, I did have a serious eye problem and when I wore glasses I could see properly.

My first experience of sex education was when I was about 11, being grabbed and pulled into her bed and held very tightly and told all about periods because I was going to a Moral Rearmament camp in Auckland. She thought something might happen while I was up there, so she told me. I didn't want to know and I didn't care. I remember her saying something. I made the remark that I would like to be a boy, then just shut my ears and lay there until she'd finished. I said, 'Are you finished?' and got out of bed. She had books but they were like everything else – underneath things. So you could get the books out but you couldn't ask questions because you weren't supposed to have them. They were really ancient books. I did know about periods, so that was okay. My sex education was confused – you put your knee up or your body is a temple – I didn't know what she was talking about, so I just thought it was another stupid thing. It was years before I understood.

As a teenager I went out with my friend Jill who lived down the road. She was allowed to have boyfriends so I went out with her and her boyfriend or in a foursome. I always got picked up from her place until my mother found out that I was going out with a particular friend. She said I mustn't go out with him, he wasn't marriageable material and she hoped that I would quickly come to my senses and marry a more suitable man. I was 17.

I could talk about all sorts of things with Jill and her mother, who didn't say I was making things up, like my mother would. Otherwise I felt totally alone, thinking about where I wanted to go and what I wanted to do, fighting for it and being told all along I couldn't do it, but doing it anyway. I don't think I ever did anything totally wrong. Everybody thought I had this very nice upbringing – church and a beautiful home, plenty of money, that sort of thing. It's made me aware that out there, people may not cope.

I did quite well at school, although the sixth form was a terrible year. There was no way I could get UE because I didn't have enough subjects – I'd done homecraft. I had to take a totally new subject and the teacher just told us to read it out of a book. That was useless, so

I had to deal with my mother and father who thought I was a complete failure because I had got School Certificate but I didn't get UE.

My father wanted me to be a librarian, but I thought that was a dead-end job. I don't know what my mother expected me to do. She clung on to me so much that I just wanted to get away and I didn't really talk about what she wanted. I decided to go nursing. When it came time to go I just made my own arrangements. I travelled to Dunedin on my own, although they did take me down the first time. I never said goodbye to her, I waved at her and watched her go away and didn't want to have anything more to do with her. It was a great relief to get to the nurses' home away from her – no more blaming sessions. But she sent me letters about what I should be doing and thinking.

I completed my nursing and worked about two weeks in a Social Welfare home as a nurse, but I couldn't cope with that. I was in tears with the children and couldn't understand myself. I got told off by the matron for being too friendly with them. She said they were diabolical people and I could see that they weren't. I used to sit on their beds talking to them – I wasn't giving them any leeway or anything but she'd come round checking and I knew I couldn't work there.

After that I worked at an old people's home which helped me grow up a bit. The people there supported me – they made me think about the old people, about their personality and that kind of thing. There was one old blind lady who was very rude, but the staff just said, 'You think about lying there not being able to see and somebody comes along and starts chatting about something. How would you feel?' It helped me a bit. They were caring people and that was a good experience.

I had met Clark by then and we got married in December 1962. It was a church wedding. Clark isn't really into that, but he went through with it. These days you wouldn't, but then there was no other way. The minister was a friend of my father's and agreed to marry us. I went along with my parents' view.

We had a few problems. I wanted to sign the register out in

front of the church because I didn't want to be kissed and hugged out the back. That just about stopped the wedding. 'Just a small table.' 'No, you can't have the altar table.' 'I don't want the altar table.' 'Well, where will we get the table from?' 'We can get a table from home.' 'Oh no, you're not bringing the table from home.' Eventually they found a table out the back and everyone said, 'Well that's nice, I enjoyed that.' The minister said, 'If your father hadn't been a really good member of this congregation, I wouldn't have allowed this.'

We were not allowed alcohol at the reception – definitely, absolutely not. Clark said he would pay for it, but no, absolutely not. My mother invited screeds of people who I might see once in a lifetime. It was just before Christmas and they all thought I was getting married quickly because I was pregnant, which was not right. We were getting married because we were going overseas, but they all sat there looking sideways at me. It was strange but if I hadn't been through that experience I wouldn't have let my daughter have what she wanted, when she wanted it. I enjoyed doing that. It was very satisfying, easy and no hassle.

We went off to Wanaka for four days for our honeymoon and then left for overseas. Mum and Dad were away on holiday when we left so the wedding was the last time Mum saw me for several years. I think in retrospect she could have made the decision to come and see me off.

When I was married Mum had less control over me than before. That was good but it was about 15 years before I realised that I was still hanging on to the hope that she might be my mother one day and that I had to accept that I couldn't really carry on like that any more. Nothing was going to change. A lot of people say, 'Just go back to your mother and say, "I'm sorry" ', but I can't. She'd either get really angry or cry and say, 'I could have been a better mother', but she wouldn't change.

Unless you've been through something like that you can't understand it. Sometimes when I'm talking to people I can spot that they've been through it all – there's an empathy there. At other times people have no idea what you're talking about. It only affects you when you're starting to overwork or when something is confronting you. When I started working at a clinic all my anger started to come out. Everything I did was directed towards my mother. After working on it for about four years I got rid of most of it.

The guilt you feel if you can't stay with your mother is awful, but then I think, 'No, I am the one who has to survive – I'm the one who has to keep going and it's important for me to feel I'm doing the right thing.' I visited Mum about a year ago. She wouldn't let me go, she hung on to me, saying, 'Don't ever leave me, I love you so much', but it's not love at all. It's exhausting and I couldn't cope with it. I couldn't have a proper conversation with her and I haven't been down since. It's difficult to get to where she lives but I don't have any inclination to go. When I was looking after old people I made aspersions about people who never came to visit. Now I have changed my mind.

When we had our two daughters I found it extremely difficult not to hit them, extremely difficult. One day when Dawn, who's very headstrong, was about two years old, she said, 'You can't hurt me, you can never ever hurt me. I don't care how many times you hit me, you can't hurt me', and she said it in such a cheeky way that if I had lammed into her I think I would have killed her. So I ran round the house about eight or 10 times, holding on to myself, until I felt better. From then on I realised I had to stop and think and recognise there were definitely other ways of doing things. Clark helped me in thinking about other ways, otherwise I would have behaved just like my mother – although I never shook the girls like she shook me. That was just awful. Even now when people hug me, it gives me a creepy feeling that they're going to do more. It's scary and I just don't like it.

I became determined that I wasn't going to be the same as my mother with my children. If they needed me, I was going to be a support. If they came to me and said something, then I would help them through it. For example, when Dawn was about five, she came home and told me a man wanted her to get in a car. I didn't say, 'Oh, how stupid.' I said, 'Where?' She told me and said, 'What should I do?' We went to her teacher who said, 'We've taken care of that –

someone else complained too.' She knew that had happened and that that man would never be there again. She was really supported through it – she didn't make it up and she wasn't being silly.

I think it's important to encourage children to tell you anything and everything, it doesn't matter whether it's good or bad. When they come home from school, turn around and listen to what they're going to say, make an appropriate comment. Don't say, 'I'm too busy', or 'I can't talk to you now.' Most of the time they just need a second. Like when Kerry was six she said in the middle of a dinner party, 'What's a homosexual?' I had made up my mind that every time she asked a question, no matter where I was, I would answer it. So I said to her, 'It's two people, not a man and a woman, it could be two men or two women, who like each other.' 'Oh, thank you. Can I leave the table now?' You don't have to go into great detail about how or where homosexuals live or what they do, just what it is. I think it was about six months later when she and Dawn came and said, 'We don't want to know anything fancy about this, but how are babies made?' They learned when they were five and seven.

We had our ups and downs when they were teenagers. I remember one night Kerry said, 'Well, you'll just have to ring them up and say you can't come to work because I need the car.' I thought, 'Hang on, this is my car!' But we sat down, the four of us with our two cars, and in the end she took me to work. She wasn't the least bit happy about coming and getting me but she did, so that worked reasonably well and I think she got the message that work is more important than play. Play is quite important but they are different. That night we did all get to the right place at the right time because we had sat down at the table and talked about it. Often I would say that they couldn't do something and Clark would say, 'Why not?' So I'd have to think, 'Why not?' He would say, 'I think they can go out, I think they'll be all right, but they must be home at such and such.' And usually I'd agree.

I have a good relationship with our daughters who have had a different way of being brought up.

Kerry got married in 1988 and she and John get on very well, they're friends with one another and that's really good. Dawn has a boyfriend. We have a house in Turangi and we all go there together and get on extremely well. They must enjoy it because they come back again, but we don't make any claim on them and they don't have to come home at Easter or Christmas or anything like that.

Dawn is a bit like her father. She's able to cope on her own. She knows what she wants to do and yet if you put a brick wall in front of her she'd just climb right over the top of it. She'd just think, 'That's a bit difficult.' That is how she reacted as a toddler.

Neither of them has children yet and there's no way that I would pressure them to have them. They can decide for themselves. I've had my children the way I wanted them and they can do what they want to. I have a sister who didn't have any children, so it's not a totally foreign thing – if there aren't any more little ones, well, that's the way it goes. It would be very nice, but it's not going to be the only satisfying thing in my life.

Although it's been difficult, where I come from is really an advantage. If you have no problems and everyone supports you along the way, you're not much help to anyone, are you?

When I was young we seemed to outsiders to be a perfect family doing perfect things. We attended church, we thought right thoughts, we did everything absolutely perfectly. I was told that as a child, but I could see that it was not like that and I had doubts about everything after that. The most important thing to me now is how I feel in a relationship. It has nothing to do with anybody outside – just how you feel with your children and your husband. And if you don't work on it, then you don't deserve it.

Kerry

My father worked for an oil company so we lived all round the world. I went to the Caribbean with my parents at the age of 10 weeks, but obviously I don't remember any of that. The part I remember most is living in South-east Asia when I was 10 and 11. We were there for just over a year and I loved it. I remember it being the most fantastic life for a child. Even going to school was fun because you met so many exciting people from other countries. They found me interesting and I found them interesting. We lived outside and got very brown and swam every day. It was beautiful but it was also a very unreal childhood experience. When I came back to New Zealand and started school here I found it so difficult. The children teased me and I was incredibly sensitive. It almost makes me want to cry now, thinking about how cruel those children were. Maybe there was a little bit of jealousy involved – maybe they'd wanted to do that sort of thing. I also spoke with a very English accent, which of course singles you out, and I think I responded to that by taking on a very Taranaki accent which I've never lost, much to my shame.

I wasn't conscious of it then, but over the years I've become more and more conscious of how much support Mum gave me as a child. She was just a rock.

There were little things. At high school I used to get glandular fever recurrently, especially over the winter, and I remember there was one particular science test that was extremely important. I was away from school for about three weeks and missed most of the classes for that test – it was something to do with the circulation of the blood in the body. I was going back to school and the day before the test my mother got out all her nursing textbooks and sat down with me and went through it all. I must admit I never considered my mother to be particularly bright or brainy – Dad was a genius to me, he knew everything – but Mum was sort of Mum and didn't know all that much. But she did! Back at school I think I got about 98 per cent in the test – the highest mark in the class. I was so proud of her doing that because she was the one who got me through.

Mum and Dad had different expectations of us. With Dad, it

was always, 'You must do this.' I think from the age of five he said, 'You have to go to university!' There was no argument or anything – 'You're just going' – and I never really questioned it. But Mum always said, 'Just do your best.' Even if something was fairly mediocre she would praise it and say it was good – she always made you feel good about it. And she still does that today.

I had a lot of arguments with my mother during my teenage years, basically because we are different people. Sometimes I find it quite difficult to stay with her and Dad, in that she says things that absolutely infuriate me. They make me want to say, 'What the hell do you think that for?' or 'Why do you say that?' I think it's just the way she's been brought up. Sometimes the things she says have absolutely no logic, so I have a problem with that. Perhaps because of that we're not as close as we could be. I like to talk to her and sometimes it clicks and we can talk together and I'll feel good about it, but sometimes I feel that she's trying too hard and I feel guilty because I'm not trying at all. I'm switched off. Mum's very good at talking to people. She used to talk to my friends, and my friends would say, 'Oh, your mother's so wonderful, she's easy to talk to', but I never found that. I would never talk to her about sex or anything like that, that was my business. I was almost too embarrassed to tell her when I got my first period. I just didn't want to tell her. That's just me, I think. Most of my other friends can talk to their Mums very easily, but I won't.

When I left school, I went to Victoria University. I applied to a hostel and was accepted and was very happy. But at almost the last moment, it seems to me, although it was probably months earlier, my parents announced they were moving to Wellington. I thought things were still under control because they planned to move to Lower Hutt so I kept the hostel place. Then when we actually came down here they found a house that was absolutely across the road from the university – in fact, the hostel was further away – so there was no excuse for leaving home. I was really disappointed.

I was ready to go but I stayed with them. In a way I think that was a big mistake, because university didn't mean anything to me. It was like going to school and it shouldn't have been. So I went flatting in my third year. Even then my father made it particularly hard for me. I don't think he wanted me to leave. He said, 'You'll be back', because the rent was quite high on the flat. But Mum was quietly there in the background saying, 'I think it will work.' I was 20. It was well past time to leave.

After what my father said, I was determined that I wasn't going back and I didn't. I had three part-time jobs. I was a housemaid at a Wellington hotel. I also cleaned the penthouse for a woman who lived at the hotel and I cleaned another house up in Wadestown. It was quite tough. I didn't get any financial support from my parents at that point but they were always there for me. Mum was always there on the phone, listening to anything I wanted to say, like, 'Hey, I'm feeling really tired', or she'd ring and say, 'Come round for a meal.'

I did politics and history and that was great. I loved history at school and I drifted into political science by accident. I thought, 'Oh, this looks interesting, I'll do it.' At the end of the first year the lecturer said to me, 'I think you've got a bit of talent here, why don't you keep going?', so I ended up doing a double major. But I always think that that was a bit of a disappointment to my father – he would have preferred something useful. But my mother's always thought it was great that I did it. Anything at university was an achievement and if I dropped out I'm sure she wouldn't have said anything, just, 'Do what you want with your life.'

I think she was doubly keen on that idea because she was working full-time herself. She hadn't really worked before we came to Wellington and I think she was probably a little bit neurotic – sitting at home you'd go stark raving mad. When she got to Wellington and started getting into volunteer work and working at the clinic she was almost a different person – so alive, going out to meetings and organising things. She was so proud of the fact that she could do this, because I think she'd begun to think that she was pretty useless. I feel so sorry for her because she seemed to have wasted all those years. I'm so lucky that I'm able to do what I want to do.

At the end of my degree I got a job for a couple of months to save money to go overseas. I went in March and returned in December. I wish it had been longer but it was probably fortuitous that it wasn't, because I was able to come back and get a job straight away. I also came back because of John. I'd met him before I left.

I must admit, during the time I was in England I didn't have much contact with my parents and that hurt me a little bit. I used to write quite a lot, I think. I'm not sure, actually – maybe I didn't. I had a perception that I wrote quite a lot and didn't get much back. I thought maybe they just didn't care, but I think what they were saying was, 'She's doing her own thing and we'll leave her alone.' Whereas when you're 21 you're still pretty immature – you still want to know there's somebody at the end of the phone who is receiving your letters and thinking about you.

My grandmother lived in England for a while and that's where I got to know her. That's why I had difficulty with my mother's story of her childhood because to me my grandmother's a lovely woman, but I probably don't know her as well as I thought I did. I stayed with her for quite a while. She always did so much for me and she reminded me quite a lot of Mum in a way – I'm sure Mum would hate me to say that – so I couldn't understand why Mum was always so down on Granny.

Mum's never been big on things that you think most mothers would be really interested in for their daughters. Other mothers are very interested in their daughters' looks and clothes and so on, but Mum was never really all that interested. She made us pretty dresses when we were little but other than that she's not into clothes in a big way. She hated baking and cooking and stuff like that so I was never into that either. I don't know how to knit. I did learn I suppose, but I don't know it now. I'm not good at any of those domestic things. If we weren't interested Mum didn't say, 'You must learn and you must be a good homemaker.' That was never a message from her.

John and I organised our own wedding. Most mothers like to organise their daughter's wedding but Mum didn't want to have a bar of it – she wasn't interested in the slightest. I said to her, 'Don't you want to do anything at all?', and she must have thought, 'Oh, maybe I ought to do something', so she and Dad arranged to print the invitations. I said, 'What about your own wedding?' and she went very cold. 'My wedding wasn't my wedding. My mother took over the whole thing and I couldn't really invite my friends. We had over 100 guests and they were all my parents' friends.' I think Mum was being very honest when she said, 'All I want to do is turn up at the church and have a nice time. This is your day and we'd like to enjoy it, but you do the organising. You do what you want – make it your day.'

We lived together before we got married and they've never said anything about that. They're not the sort of people who come out and say, 'You must not live together', or 'We expect you to get married straight away', or 'When you come and stay at our place you must sleep in separate bedrooms.' They never said anything like that, but we thought, 'Let's respect what might be their opinion', and whenever we went to stay with them before we were married we stayed in separate bedrooms and nobody ever said anything.

Mum's never put any pressure on us to have children either. We love our work and we're busy, and obviously we're just too selfish or whatever to have children at the moment. It would be just too much. I think Mum would quite enjoy it if we had children. I always thought she must have loved them, being a Plunket nurse, but she says that they are other people's children – 'I enjoy them and I enjoy giving them back.' When I have children I would like to be like my mother – I would like to try to suppress the feeling that, 'You must do the best in the world', and say, 'Just do the best you can.' I have a terrible feeling I wouldn't be very good at that.

If I had children it probably would change my relationship with Mum. We would have something else in common. I think that's probably our biggest problem – we have very little in common in terms of interests. As we get older I'm starting to find that things I'm interested in she's been interested in for ages and I always thought they were silly. Golf is one thing. I've just taken it up in the last six months and I love it, so that's something that we can go out and enjoy together.

One problem is that we've been quite a sporty family, doing a lot of outdoor activities. Mum never joined in those and I resented her for that. I always thought, 'Well, why can't you give it a go?', but

I know now why she couldn't. Besides making a fool of herself, which nobody wants to do, she wouldn't have enjoyed it, so why do it? When you're young you don't understand; you say, 'You're a piker, why don't you join in?' As I start to calm down a bit with the sporting activities and say, 'Well, there are other things in life', it's better – it's partly shared interests and partly maturity. Children would be a sort of bond, something that we've both done together.

I think I'd have to keep working after I had children, mainly because I saw what it did to my mother. Mum had to stop work when she got married and she went overseas straight away. That must have been awful, not knowing a soul. Dad was away at work all day and she didn't speak the language. I couldn't imagine anything worse. I know what I'm like even when I'm sick for a couple days. The weekend's lovely, but to spend every day in this house or in any house, I just couldn't stand it. Even to work part-time or do volunteer work, anything, but I don't think I could be cooped up with a child 24 hours a day.

Economics has something to do with it as well. In the sixties I'm sure Mum would have loved to keep working, but not out of economic necessity. These days, I know if I stopped working, we'd have a big struggle holding on to this house. We'd probably have to sell it – not that that's such a hardship; I mean, there are lots of people out there who are a lot worse off than us. But it wouldn't be easy.

I've read about women who have a very close relationship with their mothers and some of my friends are very close to their mothers. I used to think it would have been lovely to have something like that with my mother. But I don't think that any more. More often than not the mother becomes such an essential part of their lives they can't make even simple decisions without their mother being involved. Or even worse, their mothers dominate their lives and make decisions for them.

Mum set the guidelines but she allowed me lots of freedom within them, even when I did things she may not have liked. I've only come to realise this fairly recently. It doesn't mean that we'll ever have a perfect relationship, but it means I probably understand and respect her much more than I ever did when I was growing up. Hopefully that gives us something to build on for the future.

Lynda & Alison

Alison and Lynda's stories are evolutionary. Both of them decided to do things differently from their own mothers. As Lynda says, 'I often think my mother is like she is because of a reaction to her mother's hardness. To a certain extent I know I developed in the way that I did because of a reaction to my mother's selflessness.'

Alison's mother was reticent and hard-working; Alison, in contrast, is warm, outgoing and generous with her time and energy. While she has enjoyed being a wife and mother herself, she has supported her daughter's commitment to a career and, more recently, has actively helped her through a series of crises. In fact, Alison's comfort with the traditional role is precisely what has enabled Lynda to manage three small children and a frustrating medical condition, and to contemplate a return to work. Their respect for each other's skills and attributes easily bridges the gap in their life experiences.

I talked to Lynda before I talked to her mother, so their stories are presented in this order.

Lynda

I was born in 1955, the first girl in my family in two generations. I am the middle child with two brothers. I think my mother particularly wanted a girl so she was very pleased when I arrived. She can still tell me how she felt 36 years ago when she was told I was a girl. It obviously meant quite a bit to her. I don't think that necessarily translated into conscious preferential treatment, but I suspect I did get preferential treatment to a certain extent. I'm sure my parents would have tried to be scrupulously fair about everything they did – they were and still are very thoughtful parents.

I was closer to my mother than my father, probably because she was at home more and much more available to us. Dad worked long hours and left a great deal of the day-to-day parenting to Mum.

I was a great reader as a child. I was never interested in dolls and I wasn't overly interested in girlfriends or playing traditional girls' games – I found them pretty boring – so I used to stay at home a lot and I guess that threw me together with my mother. I can't remember ever having an acrimonious relationship with Mum in those early days. She was always there, always kind and gentle, she still is the most patient of women. I just wish I had a tenth of my mother's patience. My mother didn't have a particularly warm relationship with her mother and I know that Mum determined that her relationship with her children, and particularly with her daughter, would be quite different. She went back to work when I was 11 as a school secretary, so she was always there even then. That was a priority for her. She wouldn't have looked for a job if it meant that she wasn't at home for us after school. So I have this wonderful memory of a secure, stable, happy childhood.

My mother and I diverged a bit during adolescence – I think she had quite different expectations of me at that stage than I did of myself. One of the things I admire most greatly about her is that we've never really had a fight or disagreement that's caused a serious breakdown in our relationship, and that's mainly to my mother's credit. If she's annoyed with me she will perhaps go a bit quiet and not speak for a while, but she would never have great confrontations. I can think of the times that I've challenged her, like when I was an adolescent and I wanted to go to a rock concert with some boys and stay over the weekend. I was probably about 15. She said 'No' to that one, and I put on a bit of a tantrum, didn't speak for a couple of days. Then there were the other behaviours like having the odd drink, which I started at a fairly early age, or when she accidentally discovered my contraceptive pills. I must admit that she was shocked and unhappy about that, but she has always given me room to be myself, to grow, to be independent – she's just been tremendous that way. I think I did things a lot earlier than she would have expected, yet she didn't try to stop me, or chastise me, or force me into other directions. I think she took the tack that she had taught me certain basic philosophies or moralities and after that I had to make my own decisions. I hope I can be like that with my own daughters.

However, from mid-adolescence till well into my twenties, while we had on the surface a very good loving warm relationship, there were lots of things I did and thought and hoped for that she never knew about – some of which she wouldn't have understood and others I think she preferred not to know. It was the usual generation gap exaggerated by the issues of the times, the late sixties and seventies – the Vietnam War, drugs, sex, music, the new freedoms my generation experienced.

Mum felt that education was very important, partly because it was good to take advantage of opportunities but partly because she would have liked to have gone on in education herself, to have pushed herself a bit more, and she was not really encouraged to at home. So she encouraged me as much as the boys to get at least four years' secondary education. She wanted us all to get University Entrance, but when I decided to go to university that brought her up with a bit of a shock. She'd actually never thought that any of her family would go to university – nobody ever had.

My mother jokingly, but I think with a certain amount of seriousness, pictured me marrying 'the boy next door', having some children and living in the neighbourhood with her being able to pop in. I suppose more the sort of thing that had happened for her generation. Unfortunately none of that was on my agenda. I thought I was utterly uninterested in marriage and children and so on. From quite an early age I think I was a budding feminist. I was determined to get as much education as I could, a university degree first, then a career and travel the world. Plans for relationships and children were a long way off.

I was first to break up the happy family when I won an AFS (American Field Service) scholarship to America at age 17. That was the first time I really challenged my parents in what they wanted for me and what they were prepared to support me in. I know that deep down they were unhappy about it. At 17, their only daughter was leaving and they were tremendously worried. In fact it cost them quite a bit and they really didn't have much money; they went to enormous lengths to get the money for me to do something they didn't really want me to do. They could see that it was an opportunity for me to learn a lot and grow and mature – and I did all those things – and they didn't want to stand in my way.

When I came back from America, I studied at university in Auckland for a year, during which time I holidayed in Australia where I met John. I was 18. A trans-Tasman relationship developed and at 19 I said to my parents, 'I'm going to Australia to live and study and I'm going to live with this chap.' I was going to another country to a man they had met once for about two days! This was so totally at odds with the hopes and expectations they held for me at that time. Again they didn't try to stop me or talk me out of it or lay down the law and say, 'You are not going', or anything like that. They were obviously deeply unhappy about it and I know my mother wept many tears, but they knew me to be a pretty strong sort of person and they felt that if I believed it was the right thing, then they would support me. It was amazing, really amazing.

So I headed off to a strange city in a strange country and I've never been home since. So my mother, who had this image of me being there until I got married, lost me at the age of 17. I think she's always regretted that.

My mother has always been the reference point against which I've judged what I've done in my life. The values that she instilled in me – they have been what I've judged my actions against. There have been things I might have done which I haven't done because I knew it would hurt my mother. If I can instill a set of values like that in my children, I think it would be the best thing I could do.

I was in Australia for eight years and the umbilical cord was quite strong. I came back fairly frequently – fares were cheap in the seventies. And we've always written long letters, my mother and I, really chatty long letters, and tapes. That's what our relationship is like when we meet too. We chatter away, although we didn't talk about the really big things until recent years. I felt, maybe erroneously, that my mother wouldn't understand – there were issues like abortion, homosexuality, extra-marital relationships or drugs, that my friends were involved in. I guess it was partly that Mum wasn't around – maybe if she'd been there down the road, it would have come out that my friend was doing X, Y or Z, and how did we feel about that, but because our contact was fairly sporadic and only for a week or so at a time we didn't touch on those deeper issues. It wasn't really until I had kids and we started spending a lot more time together that we did talk about those things.

At first I was a social worker in Australia, then I got more into social work management, then finally I became a personnel manager. My career was vitally important to me but when I hit 30 I said to John, 'Well, are we going to have children?' It was my decision – John left it up to me. I think he wanted children but he knew it was me who was going to make most of the sacrifices. It was a difficult decision but the biological clock was ticking over. I guess I was reluctant initially but was eventually so pleased with my children I had three!

Mum was rapt when I became pregnant. We were back in Wellington by then. She came down for each one and it was really during those times, particularly after the first one, that Mum and I forged the relationship we have today. My first child had the true colic and Mum was there during all that period, for three months or so. I must have been a trial too. I don't know whether it was post-natal depression, but I took to motherhood badly. I resented the loss of my career, the loss of my freedom. I'm not very patient, unlike my mother. I get tired and bitchy, I'm a moody sort of person at times.

I really put my mother and John and everyone through hell those first months, and Mum was just like a saint through the whole thing. It was an exceptionally cold winter and we were stuck in one room; I'd bite her head off and she'd just quietly answer me back and be there and be sympathetic. She's really quite an amazing woman.

We went to live in Auckland for nearly two years when the second one, Kathryn, was two months old. This is when the help from my mother really began. I'd been having arthritic pains for years but it wasn't until I got to Auckland that I had it diagnosed as congenital hip malformation. So not long after I got to Auckland, I had one lot of surgery. My mother was living on the North Shore and we were half an hour away on the city side. My mother left my father to fend for himself during the week and came over to live with us for a month or two while I recovered. She ended up staying for nine months because I never did recover from that operation. It didn't work and I remained on crutches. During all this I decided that I wanted a third child. This is me all over: once I make a decision it's hard to deflect me from it, and I'm sure my mother doubted my sanity. So I got pregnant, thinking that I was going to get better by the time the pregnancy was on a few months. As it turned out I didn't, so I spent the whole nine months on crutches, and as I became very pregnant it became quite difficult. A couple of months before the baby was born we came back to Wellington then had the baby in a home birth. Again my mother arrived instantly. Dad has been infinitely patient about this – he's equally fond of his daughter. I must say I felt really bad about breaking up their family. She's also got responsibilities towards her parents, who are both still alive at 100 and 99.

It was fine with John, too. Again, that's another strength of my mother's. John's a very strong and dominant person and my mother's one of the few people who can really handle him. I think he thinks she's a bit of a saint. He never seems to worry at the prospect of my mother coming down. It's marvellous because she fits in so well and is so selfless.

There's an interesting point in this. I often think my mother is like she is because of a reaction to her mother's hardness. To a certain extent I know I developed in the way that I did because of a reaction to my mother's selflessness. I think we children and my father took advantage of this.

I think one of the reasons I did develop into a strong, assertive person is that I saw my mother being used, often in the nicest possible ways, being taken for granted and not being able to stand up for herself. I could see that while on the one level it's wonderful to be patient and eternally giving, on the other you don't necessarily achieve things for yourself. My mother has compromised all her life. I was determined I was going to be confident and not afraid to do things. In my early working career I pushed myself forward and did things that I had no experience in. I was often afraid but people didn't know it. I was in the public limelight a lot, involved in contentious issues.

Three weeks after my last baby was born I was called into hospital to have a hip replacement, so my mother ended up staying two months that time. And I rang her today to tell her I'm having another hip replacement. I don't want to take her help for granted and I feel guilty about asking her to leave her home and husband and other responsibilities, but she's the best person to have here. She's terrific with the kids. John and I relate to her and she seems genuinely willing. It's not that she thinks, 'It's my daughter, it's my duty', she seems to love it. My mother seems genuinely happy when she's helping people.

I think our relationship's changed through living together in close quarters and sharing the early days after giving birth. Mum has shared my physical pain, my tiredness and my frustration. We've gone through a lot of blood, sweat and tears together and it really has brought us to our current close adult relationship. It was close and good and unquestioning as a child; then there was a period when I was 'spreading my wings' when it was perhaps uneasy, although that was under the surface. Now we can talk about most things while still retaining our separate identities, views and beliefs. We wouldn't necessarily agree on all issues, but we'd have a good discussion about it, a good to-and-fro exchange. And I think both of us would be prepared to modify our views to a certain extent, depending on the view of the other person.

We don't talk a lot about our feelings for each other but I know we love each other, and I think Mum's proud of my various achievements. Mum enjoys us doing things together like going shopping and having morning tea and pottering around. And she's got a pretty good understanding of where I'm coming from. She's got very good insight into my character. I wonder that it doesn't put her off. I can be impatient, I want to get on and make things happen; my mother's more of a wait-and-see type of person.

I know if I'm ever hurt emotionally or physically, even at 36, I still think, 'Oh, I'd like my mother.' Even though I've been living with John as long as I lived with my parents, I can still feel the pull towards the nest. You hold your own daughter and give her a cuddle and you can relate to the generations of women who have done this for their daughters.

Alison

My mother was an excellent mother because she had a hard time during the 1930s Depression. She was a very hard worker. She worked in the garden, she sewed and reused everything, she made our school uniforms out of Dad's old navy blue suits, and she made dozens of patchwork quilts for the Red Cross. She was a very good mother providing the material things in life, but I don't remember her being very emotional – not too many hugs and kisses. But then not everybody can show their emotions. I think that was the way she was brought up. She had a hard life herself, oldest of 10, growing up on a farm. Her lack of emotion didn't make a great deal of difference to my sister and me because we had nothing to compare it with.

Despite the Depression, we had a very stable home life. My father was fully employed during that period. There wasn't much money, but one highlight of the year was a camping holiday in some resort in the North Island. In the 1920s women stayed at home even if they didn't have children straight away, which was quite a loss to the workforce when you think about it – must have caused a lot of frustration too – but by the 1940s it was more acceptable to work, and my sister and I worked until we had children. It was expected that women would stay home to bring up the children, this was their role, unlike today when women can continue working, with childcare and helpful partners.

The employment we could do was really limited. We could either be a nurse or a stenographer, or work in a factory or a shop. I wanted to be a Karitane nurse but you had to pay for your training and Mum and Dad couldn't afford it. My sister was a stenographer so I just fell into the same mould. I was never sorry, mind you, but I still love little babies. We didn't travel either, like young folk they do now. The war was on and we had no hope of travelling. I did all sorts of war work – I went out to Mangere to weed onions – and started to save up to go overseas with a friend but she got engaged to an airman and I met Keith and it all fell through.

As a child, I loved playing with dolls and I wanted my own

family. I couldn't wait to have children after I was married and I was quite happy when my first baby came, a son. I was very happy with my lot and I didn't really anticipate ever going back to work. But when the three children were all at school, a friend of mine left her job as a school secretary. She suggested I take the job and I thought, 'I couldn't go back to work.' But in the end I did and loved it.

I'm a fairly emotional person and Lynda and I have developed our relationship over the years. We've become more emotional together – tears when we say goodbye, but not too 'lovey dovey'. I think it started when she was born because there hadn't been a female child born on my husband's side of the family for two generations, so I was thrilled to bits I'd produced a daughter. I looked forward to dressing her and so on. She was very special, a dear little girl.

She was always a good average at school. She always said, 'I'm not bright but I work hard', and that's true, but she really has a good above-average intelligence too. She did work hard for her exams and so on, and we weren't surprised when she said she wanted to go to university.

When she was only 16 she went to America as a Field Scholar and was there a whole year. I think that was possibly the beginning of the closer relationship. I used to write every week or send a tape. I think you can say more in letters and express your feelings better. We really became quite close because she had quite a traumatic experience with her first family. I think she was happy enough with her second family but it was very, very hard for us as parents when you're a few thousand miles apart. She developed into a very independent person with a lot of courage and a determination to make her year in America a rewarding experience.

On the way home she was billeted with an Australian AFS student. They struck up a friendship and began to write. Lynda had gone to university upon her return home and just scraped enough together for a return fare to Australia at Christmas. It was there that she met John – and that was that. When she came home there were telegrams and phone calls and flowers flying across the Tasman. We were not very happy about that, because she was only 18. Anyway

John came over and we liked him. But some months later when she said she was going to live with him, it was like a bombshell. I can remember sitting on the couch crying. My husband and I talked it over and we knew if we said, 'You can't go' or 'That's it, Lynda', we could have lost all that we've got now. She knew we didn't approve, but she was going to do it anyway – she's a very strong-minded girl, my daughter, and she would have gone regardless.

So we kept the lines of communication open and I used to write regularly and send tapes. She came home as often as she could and we kept in close contact. When they decided to get married, which we were very happy about, we went over for the wedding and it was just wonderful. It really was a lovely time, a very happy occasion. If we hadn't been prepared to acquiesce to this, look at what we would have missed out on now with our three lovely little grandchildren. I feel that mothers in my age group have had to cope with the changing times more than in my mother's generation because girls and boys are going to live together. They're going to leave home, go overseas and do their thing, which we never had a chance of doing.

Lynda's a very talented girl. She finished her degree and it would have been a waste for her not to have a career. John backs her every way, all down the line. At one stage I began to think she might not have children. She had important jobs in Australia and when they came to live in New Zealand she became personnel manager in a hospital – that's a big job. And she liked it. My husband often said, 'I don't think Lynda's going to have a family.' I said, 'Oh don't be too sure, there's always hope.' I was looking forward to having more grandchildren. Anyway, time was going by and it seemed she may make a career her life. She said herself that she had to make a conscious decision to have children, because her job was developing and as time went on it would become harder to give up the challenge. When she rang up with the news, we were thrilled to bits.

Your daughters' children aren't more precious than your sons', but because of Lynda's health problems, I've cared for her three children on more than one occasion and am very close to them. Anthony's something special, of course, being her first. I went down to Wellington when he was only a few days old to help out. When

Kathryn was born I went down again to mind Anthony. Being the first granddaughter, she's something special too and she just sailed through life as a baby. She was only three months old when they came to Auckland to live for two years. I thought it was great having my daughter and grandchildren nearer. I missed the mother-daughter thing – going shopping and being able to ask, 'Do you like this, Lynda? Is this me?' Our likes and dislikes are similar. She would ring up – she hadn't made any friends in Auckland at that stage – and say, 'Are you doing anything?' 'No.' 'Can we come over?' We really had a lovely time those few months.

Then Lynda had to have an operation on her hip. She'd been born with 'clicky' hips and we hadn't known. There was no sign of it when she was growing up. We still feel bad about it. She found out that if she had the operation in Wellington she could have it done quicker. When she rang and said, 'I think I'll have to have it done,' we said, 'We'll be with you all the way. You just go ahead and have it done.' My husband said, 'If that means you going over there, that's fine. I'll cope here.' So she had the operation, and Keith and I went over for a fortnight to mind the two children until John came back from Wellington. Then I continued to go over every Monday morning and come home every Friday afternoon. I picked up my father who lives with us from my sister's, cared for him over the weekend, then reversed the procedure on the Monday morning. Kathryn was only a nine-month-old baby and Anthony was just a little toddler. I wondered if I would get overtired and not be able to cope. But I loved it. I loved being with the little children.

After the operation Lynda wasn't allowed to walk for six weeks, but that wasn't the end of it. The operation didn't work. She was in constant pain, but when she went down to Wellington for a check and had x-rays the surgeon said, 'I can't understand why it's taking so long but I think it's all right', so they went ahead and had a much-wanted third baby.

We were very sorry when the operation wasn't a success, terribly upset for them. They left here in August to go back to live in Wellington and the baby wasn't due until February. I couldn't go down. I just couldn't with my father to look after and my mother in the rest home and my own husband. He'd had a heart attack and I couldn't leave him. She coped somehow with the pregnancy. Because she was pregnant she couldn't have x-rays to see what had gone wrong with the operation, but as soon as the baby was born she did. The surgeon still couldn't see why it hadn't worked, but he said, 'We'll have to do a complete hip replacement. When would you like it done?' She said, 'I'll wait until Kristy's about six weeks old.'

When Kristy was exactly three weeks old, Lynda had a phone call to say that he had a cancellation. So she took off to hospital and I took off to Wellington, all within 24 hours. The next morning John said, 'Here's the formula. You do this, you do that', and went off to work. I got the tin of formula and worked it all out. She was a dear wee thing – so good.

The hip replacement worked perfectly, it's marvellous. But now the other leg is bad and she has to have that done. She'll have the operation in November. I'll go down then, Keith will come down in December and we'll have Christmas with them. Keith has been extremely supportive. He's exceptionally fond of his daughter and he's a very considerate father. He doesn't leave it all to me.

It isn't at all what I expected to happen to my life as I got older. I thought once the children got married that would be it. I didn't anticipate Linda's problem with her hips, I didn't anticipate my son's redundancy or his marriage breakup, and I didn't give any thought to my parents being this old. My mother will be 100 next month. You think, 'Oh well, we all die about 80 or 90 or so', but they've gone on and on, and they're both very well. They're just going to wear out and one day, of course, the old ticker will give up. So not only have we one son come home to live but we have my father living with us too, which I never ever anticipated.

Having children has brought Lynda and me closer together. When I had babies it brought to me closer to my mother, too. Up till then she wasn't very emotional but I can remember when I told her I was pregnant with my first one she burst into tears. I was so thrilled for Lynda, but my mother cried. Not that she wasn't pleased. I suppose she was thinking of all you go through. Obviously I didn't know anything about that, but I thought she was peculiar. I did have a difficult time with the first, too. So I went to a relaxation class when pregnant with Lynda and everything was entirely different. Of course I was thrilled to have a daughter as well as a son, when she arrived.

Lynda and I can talk about anything and everything. She paid me the compliment once of saying there was never a time in her life when she didn't know the facts of life. So I must have coped with that as she was growing up. I think we just grew closer because we could express our feelings. We didn't always agree, mind you, but basically our tastes are similar. Our relationship is good – not too wishy-washy. When she was living in Australia and went back after holidays, tears were shed on both sides, but now we can part quite unemotionally because we know we'll be seeing each other again in a few months' time.

I like the way she copes with life. She's always coped well. Anything she's gone into she's done well. She's got on with her life and made it work. She sticks up for herself and has a strong personality. She used to argue with her father who has a similar personality. He used say, 'You shouldn't be arguing like that.' I said, 'Well, they're taught to express themselves in school and she can't have two standards.'

I quite understand her wanting to go back to work. I don't mind if she does, because I know her personality would be warped at home and she will make sure she has got adequate baby care. She keeps her home beautifully, it's always clean and she's always buzzing around – she surprises me the way she cooks and bakes and entertains. But that's not her entire life. That doesn't keep her fulfilled.

I admire Lynda because she gets on with it. She's president of the local Plunket, she's taking a course at Massey and they've bought a section in the Wairarapa. She takes the children here, there and everywhere; she's interested in Anthony's school work and little Kristy will never miss out. She's busy, busy. You can't help but admire a person like that, even if she is your own daughter, and I love her.

Ruth

Ruth's mother is not well enough to be interviewed but, fortunately for me, Ruth was keen to share her appreciation of her mother's life. Fortunate, because my interview with Ruth turned out to be one of the most entertaining experiences I had in the course of compiling this book. It took place after a splendid lunch for six, accompanied by fine wine and excellent conversation. Ruth's mother was there, so was her niece, and a couple of neighbours dropped in as well. The neighbours' son came in later for coffee, and as time went by I saw my interview vanishing into the afternoon haze. But the visitors drifted off and we began. I soon realised that the lunch was a typical example of Ruth's generous style. She lives alone but has a myriad obligations and friends. Sometimes obligation and friendship overlap. Her mother is a case in point – Ruth considers her a friend, but also feels a sense of responsibility towards her now that she is confined to a wheelchair. Following a series of strokes, Ruth's mother lives in the Mercy Hospital and is dependent on others for most of her everyday needs. Although she now finds it hard to maintain a conversation and cannot rely on her memory, her spirit is strong. So is Ruth's love and respect for her, as the roles have reversed and the mother has become dependent on the child.

Ruth

My childhood was pretty tough. My Dad died when I was four, and because kids never went to funerals in those days, I think for years and years we kids didn't believe that he was dead. We thought he'd gone away and hadn't come back. When you first go to school, kids ask, 'Where's your father?' 'I think he's dead.' 'You don't know?' That's pretty tough when you're just starting out.

Mum and Dad had only just moved into the house at Mt Roskill when Dad died, then Mum's Mum and Dad came and lived in the house and a great-aunt as well. I was the only girl at home and I had to help with my Gran and Grandpa, my great-aunt and my Mum. When my grandparents died one after the other, I had no idea what it meant. Grandma died – so what? Grandpa died too – so what?

It was darned hard for Mum to get everyone into school and on their way. We were all Heritage children so the boys were shipped off to board at Dilworth School, with the exception of my youngest brother who was a day boy. Heritage was a scheme for the children of servicemen and it provided education for boys but not girls. I don't think they thought girls really needed an education then, and anyway, there was no place for girls to go.

So I went to Balmoral Intermediate and Mt Roskill Grammar. I was a house captain and a prefect and I just loved sport. Scholastically I don't think I was any slouch but nobody ever directed me. I don't think we got the teachers who took an interest in us, but I didn't help matters either because I only wanted to play sport. I had one very special teacher, Miss Lily Trowern. She was kind of strange but she recognised kids with 'flair'. She spent time with me, pushed me to compete, bullied me to excel. Pity I didn't appreciate it at the time and she's now dead.

I left school at 15. I got a job at Arthur Yates during the school holidays and never went back to school. Mother wasn't too happy about it. She wanted me to stay at school but I wanted to earn money because I wanted to have 'things'. I remember her going to

Arthur Yates and the guy there telling her it was a good thing and to give me a chance. She let me stay.

I think I was quite strictly brought up, but then I can understand that Mum was probably quite worried about what was going to happen to us. I don't think I had the freedom that other kids had. When I was a teenager we argued about going out. It was the only thing we really had a toss over. She used to think the boys could look after themselves better than me!

I had my twenty-first birthday at home, then I wanted to go flatting and found a flat. I found it very difficult to tell Mum I wanted to leave home. I didn't have enough freedom, but that wasn't Mum's fault, that's the way life is. I wanted to have a boyfriend. I wanted my house and to have things my way. I wanted a kitchen. At that stage I was going to get married and have children – I don't suppose anyone really expected me to do anything else. I certainly didn't. I always dreamed that someone would buy me a nice house with a really lovely kitchen. But that didn't happen and I'm still struggling with a hopeless kitchen!

Mum didn't think I was old enough to leave home but I went and lived by myself, which I think said quite a lot about where I wanted to be. I'd always lived in a full household – 15 people to dinner, that sort of thing – and I just wanted to be by myself. I couldn't stand all those people round all the time.

Mum missed my help when I left, although I still went home for dinner every Sunday night and did the vacuuming and stuff like that. Everybody came home on Sunday nights – the boys and their wives and children. Mum always cooked wonderful dinners, like huge lamb roasts and the most glorious pavlovas oozing with cream and bananas and strawberries. They were wonderful. It'd take you an hour to do the dishes after dinner.

Like everybody else in those days, I had two jobs. During the day I worked in a sharebroker's office, where I learned all about the sharemarket and business, and in a coffee shop at night. But I decided I wanted to be in the fresh air so I left there to go apple-picking in Nelson and it was like leaving Mother all over again. I knew she didn't like it and I felt guilty. I don't believe that Mum ever told me not to do anything but I knew that sometimes I went against her wishes. I had to, because I had to grow, but it was hard for me because my brothers were all doing quite conventional things. I'm the unconventional one in the family.

The next trip was to England. I was in love and it wasn't going anywhere, so I suddenly announced I was going to England. It really was quite off the wall, like saying, 'Well, it doesn't really matter anyway because I'm going to England.' 'When are you going to England?' 'In a month.' Now England had never even entered my brainwaves until that split second, but having said it, I went. And Mum was good about that because it was like going home and I saw her family, people she'd never met.

We wrote to each other every week while I was in England. I remember that Mum would get so wound up in her letters she'd tell me a great long story and not tell me who she was talking about! We had quite a close relationship but I wouldn't say we were good friends. I don't think I had any idea who my mother really was. Part and parcel of that was not knowing the story of my father – Mum has hidden the facts of his mysterious death in 1953 for 30 years, in case it damaged us children. * It might have made life easier for her if we had known. She could have shared it a bit. All our friends knew, all their children knew, but not one person divulged it to us. Is it any wonder that I wholly support freedom of information and the truth!

Mum was having a good life then – the years when we kids grew were better for her, she had a bit of independence. She began to play croquet and she was a great croquet player, she loved it.

I went away again and it wasn't till I came back from working in America about five years later that I noticed how old and frail Mum had got. I had noticed the letters were getting very vague and I talked to my brothers, of course, who told me that things really weren't too good.

It was a hard time for Mum because it became obvious that she couldn't live in the house any more because she couldn't manage on her own. It all happened very quickly – we had to move her from the

* It is uncertain whether Ruth's father died as a result of an accident or foul play.

house to a flat. Then she got sick and had to go to a home in Hillsborough Heights. That was one of the most difficult things I've ever had to do because Mum didn't want to go and that was that. We really had to say, 'Mum, there is no choice.' She was glad afterwards because it gave her tremendous security but it was awful for us.

I went away again when Mum was at Hillsborough Heights. I called in to see her and she was very sad, but in spite of that she said, 'Go.' I was going for 12 weeks which stretched to several years. While I was away she had a very bad stroke and ended up in Greenlane Hospital. My brothers rang and said, 'You'd better get home as fast as you can', so I did and had five weeks at Mum's bedside, of which she has no memory at all. That was a very, very tough time. I had nowhere to live. I'd rented my house and ended up staying at the hospital, which was probably not a very smart thing to do because I never got a break from it. For weeks on end I sat with her and talked with someone who didn't even know me. That was scary, really scary.

Then my sister-in-law got her into the Mary Agnes wing of Mercy Hospital, thank heavens. The old people's homes we looked at were just diabolical. The fact is that Mary Agnes is for terminal care – you get a place when somebody dies. She's been there nearly three years now and we take her out every week. My brother and I share it because she's not staying there every week, that's all there is to it. There's very little recognition of the quality of age and it's awful being in the same place day after day after day. The sheer pleasure that lights up Mum's face when you get her in the car and she's got the wind blowing through her hair and a nice fresh dress on is wonderful. Every day's a blessing. We usually try to go and see one of my brothers if we're out and about, but the thing she likes best is just driving, moving around.

My relationship with Mum has changed enormously. I feel a lot more responsible now, but I never thought I'd be pushing her round in a wheelchair. When Mum was first sick the family was very united – we are a pretty tight family anyway – but my older brother and I deal better with her present situation. Let's face it, there's something funny about having to put your Mum on the toilet. Especially for me, because I'm the only one who's not a parent.

Compared with Mum I'm privileged. I've been in a situation where years before my time I've been able to earn a decent salary, and with zilch education, that's not bad going. But the main reason my life is completely different from my mother's is because I didn't have four little children dependent on me. Perhaps subconsciously I don't want to put myself in that position either. I could easily have had children as a solo mother if I'd desperately wanted them, but I guess somewhere deep down I thought, 'God, it's just the biggest sentence.' Yet I love the kids and I think the kids love me, but I'd rather be an aunty than a mother. I think that motherhood is just too tough.

There's no secrets between Mum and I now, no gameplaying, it's upfront – Mum's obviously not waiting for me to get married. And I've become a lot more patient. We talk about everything. It's a very cleansing time for us both. How lucky I am to be privy to the fears, the inner workings of the woman who brought me into this world. To be honest, I feel ashamed that I wasn't a lot more understanding earlier on, but you're not, are you? You're zooming along trying to figure out what the hell you're going to do with your life and you don't stop and think about your Mum and Dad. I count myself very lucky that we have had this time. We got it by default and we have both used it well. She is the most important person in my life and I don't have an ounce of doubt that she has taught me to be strong, courageous and proud.

Pat & Marian

Whether they want to or not, mothers and daughters rarely have a relationship unaffected by other members of the family. By focusing on mothers and only one of their children, this book creates an artificially simple picture. Sometimes that doesn't matter. In the case of Pat and Marian it probably does, because of the significance of their husband's and father's drinking. He is a silent player in both their stories.

Feminism also has an active presence, affecting mother and daughter in different ways and providing a kind of bridge across the gap between them. Marian has made informed and active choices all her life, particularly in relation to childbirth, childcare and work. Trapped for a long time in an unhappy marriage, Pat has only recently taken life into her own hands. She is enjoying exploring new ideas and becoming her own person, and she has developed a strong relationship with her granddaughters.

Pat

I was born under one mountain, Taranaki, and grew up under another, Te Aroha. Dad had just come back from the war. He was a military man and he was our commander. We had to jump to his orders. He worked as a surveyor and I used to love going out with him. We were very poor because he was always under threat of losing his job.

Mum had been a bank clerk and a very independent sort of woman, but once she got married she was really under Dad's thumb and that was that – it was tea at six o'clock on the dot, the children had to be quiet, and so on. Mum just had one baby after another which she didn't really want – six altogether, four girls and two boys.

Being the second to oldest, I was always having to do jobs for the babies as they came along. I really learnt to be a little mother quite early. When I was 11, Mum got pregnant with the youngest one and I was upset. I remember saying, 'I'm never going to have a baby.' Mum laughed and laughed and said, 'You won't be an empire builder then.' I went to see her when she had the baby and she was sitting up in bed bright as a button with this dear little baby beside her. I think I changed my mind then! I thought she'd be almost dead.

I got on well with her and I've modelled myself on her all along. She was a good listener and really very spiritual. She never talked about God but somehow she was a good example in that way. She was very religious and active in the church and that was important to me.

I went to school in Te Aroha. When I was about 15 and in high school I walked home the mile that we lived from the school and a man must have followed me. That night he attacked me in my bed – he hit me on the head. Yes, it was horrible all right, but in those days you had to put it out of your mind. There was no counselling, no therapy, no nothing. You just had to pull up your socks and get on with it. Well, I couldn't get on with it. I couldn't sleep, my school work suffered and I was sent to New Plymouth Girls' High, which was wonderful after being in a little district high school.

When I left school, I went to training college up in Auckland and stayed for a third year specialising in teaching music. It was marvellous living away from home. It wasn't a very happy home. Dad used to hit the boys and growl at Mum all the time, putting her down. I was happy to leave, although I had benefited from being in a stable family with committed parents who taught me the value of co-operation, loyalty, kindness and consideration of others.

I met my husband while I was still at school. We both trained at the Air Training Corps, and when he went overseas I took a teaching job near Rotorua. As soon as the war finished we got married and went to live on his father's farm. I was 22. It was a bit of a culture shock but I was so in love that nothing else mattered. I was virtually a townie and to go out there was a real change. All summer I'd be baking scones in the heat to take out to the haymakers. It was really boring intellectually. If I hadn't had 'Feminine Viewpoint' on the radio when I was raising my kids I would have gone mad.

I had children straight away. After a couple of miscarriages Marian arrived. I wrote a poem when she was born.

Firstborn

A quiet baby in the womb
waiting to be born
ready for the world.
Urgency transmitted, all-pervading,
I focus totally on the act of giving birth,
experience the pain and darkness.

Then by morning I see
The tiny perfect child – born of me.

After that I had a baby every two years. It was my choice in a way. Having only daughters didn't make any difference to me, I was only worried for my husband. He didn't say anything but I know he wanted a son more than anything else. It was the people round us who put the pressure on. The farmers, saying things like, 'You won't have much of a footy team', or 'You poor thing, all those weddings to pay for.' The girls often heard comments like that and later one of them said, 'I grew up thinking I was a second-class citizen.' That hit me like a blow in the face because I thought I'd encouraged good self-esteem. I'd always encouraged them to think well of themselves.

I didn't see much of Mum over that time because we were on the farm and they were down in the South Island, although we never lost touch. There'd been a tragedy in the family – one of my sisters got pregnant and Mum and Dad virtually went into shock and retirement. They couldn't face anybody in Te Aroha at all so they took off and went down south.

In the fifties we left the farm and my husband began a new job. Because of the isolation, living in the country with no near neighbours, we were a close-knit family. I was always there when the children came home from school, and we would always share our day. The children gave me the only emotional support I had, except for one good friend, a teacher who lived nearby. The girls all helped – Marian helped especially with the babies and I heard awful stories later about how she punished them with threats of what she'd do if they didn't do what she told them!

The exciting times then, when Marian was about 10, were going out in the boat in the weekend. There was usually more fish than we needed and my husband would smoke the rest for later. It was a good healthy life. We gorged ourselves on whitebait, had milk straight from the cow, watercress from the river, mullet from the river mouth and flounder as well. We made friends with our nearest neighbours, a Maori family whom we came to love. The mother had reared many children, worked hard, fought poverty and became a lonely figure who remained for many years on the periphery of my life. When she died I went to her tangi at Tahuna marae.

When my youngest daughter was born it was hard for everyone. I had been ill beforehand and finished up in National Women's Hospital, which then consisted of old army barracks. She was so tiny when she was born that she spent some days in an incubator and when I left hospital she had to stay there until she had gained enough weight (six and a half pounds) to come home. Friends and relatives helped with the others. However, she proved very difficult to rear and was in delicate health for four or five years, so I depended a lot on the two eldest children to keep things going. I've always been grateful for their support. It's not surprising that the older children matured early – they became 'little mothers' when still quite young, just as I had done. They have learnt to be responsible adults.

At this stage their father became really special to them as he was so seldom at home. I was the one who had to discipline when necessary and carry on when exhausted and stressed. His business was proving very successful and took most of his time. He began drinking too much, sometimes starting at midday, or carrying on until late at night. Once when he hadn't got home at 2 am I went down to his workplace and found him unconscious in the bottom of the boat.

In spite of this we survived as a family fairly well. I was one of those mothers who thought they hid their unhappiness and never cried in front of the children. A friend said to me recently, 'My mother didn't fight, she wept.' Well, I didn't fight either and I only cried in private.

Marian did well at school and at 16 went to training college, then later on to varsity, winning a studentship. That meant she was already independent. I was so proud of her! When she married and left home I missed her a lot, as I did all the others.

By that stage the girls wanted me to leave my marriage but I said I couldn't. One daughter said to me, 'Why not?' I said, 'Because I took my vows in church.' She said, 'Yes, but he broke the contract.' That was what triggered me, that very statement. So I thought, 'I will', and I did. Nobody else needed to say anything, that was sufficient. They had all left home by then.

Everything changed for me when I left my husband. The first huge change was experiencing group therapy with other women. There was Al-Anon which I went to every week for three years and still use. Then there were personal growth classes with Iris Barrow and others at Manukau Technical Institute. Books came into my hands and I was hungry for them. I went to eight different classes and began to rediscover myself. It took time and effort but gradually I regained strength. Later my family and some single women friends joined me in a simple ritual celebrating my freedom. It seemed right for me to do this, in spite of the fact that I wept a lot during the celebration! I've enjoyed the changes I've made, and once when Marian said, 'You could be a witch, Mum', I took it as a compliment.

I spent three years studying music therapy, met overseas tutors, made interesting friends, read widely, worked with handicapped children for four years, using music to communicate. Finally I learnt that it was probably music which kept me sane through the worst times. But there was more trauma to come. My husband went straight into the arms of another woman. That didn't bother me, but I hadn't bargained on seeing my daughters making friends with the new woman. One Christmas when I joined the family for a shared meal, I felt rejected when Marian looked up briefly from a conversation with her, greeted me, then went on talking to her as though I didn't exist. Another daughter and the grandchildren helped me through it by running to the car and helping me with the food I'd brought. The new woman is now part of our family and I am able to feel okay with her.

Part of the Al-Anon programme, which is for the family or friends of the alcoholic, is to detach with love. It takes skill and compassion to detach enough so that both mother and daughter can feel okay.

Marian and I don't ring each other or share much at all. On the other hand we do see each other fairly often with children's birthdays and things like that. She knows that I lead a pretty good life. In fact she says I am a model to her of a person who can lead a good life alone. I have a lot of affirmations from her children and her husband. I've become autonomous in my own way. Often I would like her help but I wouldn't ask because I think she's got enough on her plate. I'd like her to do things like help work out my financial situation and make important decisions. But in our family we work on the principle that you say if you need something. We don't offer help. We've got past that rescuing thing, so we don't rescue each other, unless one of us asks for help. But I don't feel comfortable asking. I think I'm probably as fiercely independent as my own mother and grandmother were.

One of the things Marian and I share is that we are both scholars in a way, both feminists too. Going to Women's Studies did that for me really. I was living in Auckland then so I could go to classes. I found I was talking the same language as her. She'd read all these books and had friendships with interesting feminists. I love to feel I'm in there with her. We do talk the same language.

I have been lonely here at times, but I now appreciate the friendship of grandchildren. One of them said to me the other day, 'I don't think of you as old, Grandma.' That was lovely. So it's become more a granddaughter closeness than a daughter one. I'm aware that my children are going through a very busy time in their lives, and a stressful time too, and there's only so much of it I can take. I walk away. They've all got friends and support networks.

I think they've noticed a big change in me and they respect me more than they did. I suppose the main difference between my own marriage and that of my daughters is that I felt I had no choice and remained trapped in my situation, whereas they did have choices and were able to exercise them. While I thought it was a good, peace-keeping thing to be passive, my daughters realised it was not. None of them have remained doormats in their marriages.

I think our relationship will change as we all get older and I think it will be for the better. Last week while walking in my garden I looked at a young pittosporum which had doubled its height in one year and thought, 'Yes, the relationship is like this tree – strong, healthy and best left alone.' So it's a more mature and stable thing where we keep our own space and allow for an ebb and flow. My strongest feelings are of gratitude and respect for what Marian's taught me, for being reliable and kind, and for managing her own life well.

Marian

I had a very good relationship with Mum, growing up. It was quite stressful because my father drank a lot and I always used to worry about his drinking. I was the oldest of a family of five girls. My second sister was a real hard case – always in trouble, really difficult. That was something of a burden because I felt responsible, being the eldest. I didn't try to change her, but I worried a lot about her: why wasn't she better behaved! We used to torment my third sister dreadfully. We had good times but we were also quite nasty to each other sometimes too. Mum provided an interesting, child-centred home environment, even though I think she was stressed and unhappy in her marriage.

At school I took 'male' subjects – physics and chemistry and maths. That was my choice. I felt very comfortable with the male teachers. Some really nice, relaxed teachers took those subjects, that's why I chose them. And I wonder in retrospect whether I was unconsciously trying to impress Dad – being the eldest, with him badly wanting a son, ignoring us all the time and not being there for us. That could have influenced me but I wasn't aware of it at the time.

I found those subjects quite hard. Again you don't realise it at the time but the whole structure of knowledge and the way it is organised is very male. Later on when I was at Ardmore Teachers' College, I took history because it was the only subject that fitted in with my timetable and I did really well in that. So I might have enjoyed the arts more.

My teenage years were okay but there was conflict around me going out with boys and Mum worrying sick about that – what were they doing to me? Maybe that went back to her own family experiences of out-of-wedlock pregnancies.

And I got into trouble – I got suspended from Ardmore Teachers' College because I had a boy in my room at 10 to 11, or something ridiculous like that. We'd been to the pictures and he came in for coffee afterwards. The College took on the parental role of being responsible for the girls – the boys were allowed to do what they liked, but a female student had to be in early. It was just a week's suspension but the friend who was with me found it quite traumatic; it was easier for me. I left home at 17 to go to teachers' college. I didn't think it was particularly young, and Ardmore was really like a home away from home – even the laundry was delivered to you. It wasn't a big transition because it was live-in. It was a very protected environment and very authoritarian, so I wasn't particularly happy there.

After being brought up in the country where everyone knows everybody else, and being very protected, it was quite a big step to go to Auckland University with its huge impersonal classes. I felt quite isolated and like a fish out of water there, but I moved into O'Rorke Hall for a while and again the group environment was quite comfortable for me.

It wasn't expected that I would go to university, no way. What happened was that I did very well with my schooling. I learned to read and write and spell very quickly so I was promoted a class – I was the youngest person even in the class behind me. Because I was so much younger than everybody else, school was quite a battle, but I decided to take it further. I don't remember getting any encouragement from Mum or what she thought about it.

I think it was Dad who put a huge pressure on us to achieve. He gave us conditional love – we were only good if we achieved. It was a huge thing for me to do two degrees and a diploma. I did two years full time and all the rest was part time. I probably wouldn't have had the energy if I hadn't had to strive to be recognised or to get approval. At least it's given me good qualifications! Although they're not the answer to everything, they are useful in validating any statements I'm making. They give me that confidence in debating, particularly with Social Welfare and situations like that.

I used to come home quite often during the weekends, particularly at college, but also at university. But I also wanted to get away. I'd been brought up in the social environment of South Auckland, and I had this huge need to get as far away from it as possible. The whole attitude towards women is just so awful in a small country town. They degrade you in every way: the man-worshipping attitude, the 'ha ha' jokes, the men going off to the pub and talking about 'going home to the old bag', that sort of thing. It was very damaging for Mum's generation. I think she must have felt unhappy and isolated and unsupported living in a community like that.

I went teaching for two years after I finished university and I got married during that time. I was 25. I left home when I got married, I suppose, in the sense of having my own life and doing my own thing. Although we often acted in a conditioned way – we used to go and see both sets of parents at Christmas and things like that – we lived our own life. We had quite a busy social life, playing bridge and having dinner parties, before we got bogged down with children.

Once I got pregnant I understood for the first time what Mum went through when she was pregnant – I remember her being in a bad mood and things like that. It gave me an understanding of how awful it is to be a mother. I found it quite stressful visiting Mum with the children because my second boy was very overactive and had a lot of problems. He'd always be getting into things and making a mess. I was supposed to keep him on a diet and Mum would give him a cup of milk which he wasn't allowed to have. So when the kids were little it was quite stressful. If I'd had nice little daughters who sat still and didn't get into things, I think it would have been better. It's easier now because the children can relate well to her and there's not those stresses, although I find now with a 40-hour working week and running a home with four kids, I get hardly any social life to go visiting. I see one of my sisters quite a lot because we cross over in our working life, but I saw Mum more often in the early days.

I worked as much as I could manage all the time I was having children. I worked when my first child was 18 months; I got a friend to mind him. Then I got pregnant again and had a year off. When I did more work at the end of that year, my husband minded them. When I got pregnant with Rosie I only managed 10 weeks' work. I couldn't run two pre-schoolers and be pregnant with a third child and work as well – it was a bit much. So my husband got a full-time job again, and I retired gracefully. When my fourth child was about

18 months old I started doing part-time work again. Mum and I weren't particularly close over that time so I don't know what she thought about me working. We never discussed it.

I find it quite boring looking after children. Some mothers like to do things with them, but I might be like my father in that regard: I get bored with just being in the company of children. I like to have stimulation. I also like to earn money. I don't like being poor. However, I did home-school them – two years with the first one and one year with the second. The oldest one was very miserable at school. He absolutely hated it. When I was miserable at school I didn't say anything, I just kept it to myself, but my children are more assertive, so we had to accommodate them. Home-schooling was intellectually stimulating for me because I learned with the children. I didn't give them lessons around the table – we went off and did things. It fitted the children's needs and it fitted mine in a way; it made my mothering more professional. I used to take the oldest one down to Mum's sometimes and he'd have the day there, so Mum actually helped me in the home-schooling, which was good. Otherwise I didn't have much contact with her.

Women's issues hit me in the face when I had my first child. Being a psychologist I was quite worried about having a baby, because I thought, 'How will I get any intellectual stimulation from all the cabbages that make up the suburbs?' But I was quite surprised when I went to a La Leche meeting and met women who were far more stimulating to talk to than any of my colleagues in the service. It was quite a revelation. I got quite involved in La Leche and at one level that was very empowering. It also gave me permission to parent in a way that I intuitively felt was right for me.

My beliefs about child-rearing centred round breastfeeding and home birth. There's a big gap between Mum's generation and mine in what we think about that. My home birth was very radical for Mum and I think she had reservations about it. I also breastfed my children until they were three, and in Mum's day babies were weaned at nine months or sometimes a year. That was a women's issue because all those ideas came from Truby King. I had moved on to feed in a different way. It was an issue about authority too. I didn't necessarily reject authority but I was critical of the doctors, and thought they were lacking in knowledge about some things. That was very different to Mum's generation where the doctor was somebody you trusted and respected. There was a big gap between us.

There are other effects of having a home birth and breastfeeding. When you're breastfeeding, your body is changed radically. And when you have a home birth you feel that *you're* doing the birthing, you don't hand yourself over at the hospital door and have things done to you. The home birth gave me self-confidence and a belief that I was a strong competent person. The same with breastfeeding – a sense that my body was okay. It's part of this quite deep feeling about yourself. Mum had four-hourly schedules and things that her babies had to conform to; if I had that I wouldn't have had enough milk to feed my babies. The basic integrity of my body would have been put in question.

I found my emotional support came from the women friends I made through La Leche, and I got support from the home birth people also. I share things with my next sister, but not with my other sisters or with Mum. Because women friends have been through the same struggles, you actually get quite close. You're on the same wavelength and you've got the same problems – like juggling work and home and little moans about the demands of a partner having to play the wife for a while.

With the mother-daughter relationship, the most important part is during pregnancy and childbirth and in the early years. I sacrificed a lot for my daughters in terms of tiredness and I try to meet their needs absolutely now. I get on well with them, but I don't see an awful lot of them because of the hours I work. I sit and have tea with them, then they're off to do their own thing. The mother-daughter bond is most vital in that early period in terms of closeness and connections. After that you always have a special bond with your mother, but I feel it's more appropriate to seek emotional support outside.

I don't know where my daughters get their emotional support from. They probably get it from their girlfriends. They're at the stage where they shut their doors and things like that. When I'm at home there's not normally a lot of time to be together, so they just go about their daily lives. My husband tells me that if I go down to Wellington or anything like that, they always ask how long I'll be and when I'll be back, so they obviously do care, but they don't show it in any way. Whenever they get very sick they'll come back to me, but they are certainly centred on their friends rather than me, so I feel that their primary relationship isn't with me any more. Even though they're only nine and 12, they seem to be completely independent.

I think I've developed my emotional side from having the children. I've also had marriage troubles and things like that, so I've got to know my anger and violence. I feel that I've got many of my qualities from Mum and I'm just pioneering my own way with them. Mum gave me good basic mothering so I've got that emotional security which is really something. The nurturing side comes from her too, although I don't know whether I am a good mother or not. I don't even think about it. You develop intuitive patterns.

I was brought up with all girls in the family and it's very interesting for me having two sons and then two daughters because I feel quite differently towards my daughters than I do towards my sons. Quite differently. Rosie will still sit on my knee or I'll stroke her hair. I'll kiss Juliette – she's nine. There's been cuddling from childhood, that sort of touch has never stopped, whereas Gregory was quite young when he told me not to touch him. He said, 'Don't kiss me any more.' The boys and I don't have that same physical closeness. They have their own space round them that I'm not to enter. It's not that the girls are overly coy, but it's okay for me to stroke and braid their hair while it's not okay for me to stroke Gregory's hair.

I don't think we were really touched much as children. Mum always had a baby in her arms. We didn't ever use terms of endearment or hugs unless someone was in distress. She was a good caring mother but she didn't show affection in that way. I felt some of my mothering style came from my grandmother. She was a bit difficult but I admired and respected her and I have some of her 'hardness' if you like. Mum actually seemed to enjoy playing with the kids, but I never did and I often wonder whether I got some of that from my grandmother.

I got my social awareness about issues and things like that from Mum too. And a consistency – I won't be sidelined by anyone. In a lot of my schooling I challenged the accepted way and got myself into trouble by taking up issues around feminism and things like that. That probably came from my mother's mother as well as Mum. My grandmother was into sticking up for things – once she wrote to the town clerk about a clock being pulled down – and she cared about fairness. The concern with social justice definitely comes from Mum's side of the family. And I've got an appreciation of music and artistic things from Mum. If my life was different I'd like to develop that side of me.

My life's radically different to Mum's. It's a different awareness. When I got married I was very careful to marry a man who wasn't like my father. I wanted to have my own life, I didn't want to be just the wife. I could actually choose and get a quality of life. In Mum's time that was almost impossible. If I'd been brought up in Mum's situation I would probably have hit the bottle or something. It must have been very depriving being there just to service your husband and your children.

Another thing is that I can earn a good wage. I had a real battle with my husband to be able to go back to work. He didn't want to work part-time and share parenting responsibilities. I got really stroppy and he found that really hard. We went off to counselling about it and the counsellor was somebody who was off work while his wife was earning the income. That was a good choice because he gave my husband 'permission' to do it, if you like. Changing roles like that was radical when I did it – it would have been impossible for Mum. She would probably have been put in Carrington or Oakley or somewhere if she'd suggested it. It was just not on. The choices weren't there.

Elizabeth & Frances

While the social changes that have occurred over the last 50 years have benefited women as a whole, they have also created a distance between the generations.

Elizabeth is a career woman with a demanding but highly satisfying job and no children. She has consciously chosen a life that is different from her mother's, and lives in an era when having a career is not only possible but widely accepted. Her mother, Frances, was an adventurer before she married, but gave up her adventures and her career to care for her children, exploring new avenues only when they were grown. Although the differences in their lives mean they have to work harder to maintain their closeness, a strong link remains between them. They can and do count on each other in a crisis.

Elizabeth tells her story first.

Elizabeth

Mum was a fantastic mother for a child to have. She was intelligent, so she always helped us with our homework. She was well educated herself – with English assignments she had always read the novels we were studying, we could talk about the poetry and she would have ideas – intellectually it was excellent. I had a really good high school education, but it was partly the input from my parents that made it good.

She never worked outside the home while we were at school, apart from occasionally picking fruit at the orchard and earning a bit of pocket money. She was always home when we were home so she was always available for us. I really value that and I think that gave me a really good grounding and a real confidence that I could do anything. There was a security there and I am quite sure it was a good emotional investment.

My father and mother had a really harmonious relationship so my tolerance for stress and conflict is pretty minimal. They gave us a really pleasant, calm and peaceful environment so I can't cope with loud noises and shouting. I think in some ways that's a disadvantage because a good healthy bit of conflict and noise and argument is good, but my tolerance levels for that are pretty low. I like peace and quiet.

I left home at 17 to go to university and probably from that point started to develop quite a different idea of what I wanted for myself. Being female I was reasonably mature, but I did quite a lot of growing up on my own over that time.

Mum had been to university and I think it was always assumed that I would go. I suppose in those days it was really a way of deferring getting a job, and I didn't choose subjects to get me in a certain position. I now make decisions about where I want to be in a much more conscious way. I didn't do that back then because I didn't have ambition – no, not ambition, that's not the right word, but it took me a long time to feel that I could influence my destiny and do things for myself.

I stayed in a hostel for a time, but didn't like it. I'm not a hostel person so I soon went flatting. I met Mike reasonably quickly after that and lived with him for a while. Mum and I didn't ever specifically talk about that, we didn't discuss it – it just happened and was accepted. Mum had lived in mixed flats in London and I felt I had a Mum who had done a lot of those kinds of things early on. She had quite an unusual life compared to most of my friends' mothers. She hitch-hiked and bicycled through Europe and we had photographs of her from the Dutch newspapers and on the back of trucks, travelling in the days when it wasn't so common for Kiwis to go overseas. I think it must have been just after the war, and it seemed to me that pre-us she'd had a really exciting life and done a lot of things. She travelled a lot, she was attractive and outgoing, and at some point I must have sensed the comparison with what her life was now, although she never ever complained.

I used to go back home for the long vacation for the three years I was at varsity, but I always had to work to earn money so I don't know how much company I was. I used to talk to Mum quite a lot about my work but probably not a lot about relationships. When I say we're close, what do I mean? I think we were really close during my school years, but leaving home when I was 17 I had to deal with a lot of emotional stuff alone or with friends. I didn't talk about those things with Mum because quite often they weren't problems by the time I went home – the matter had been resolved. I think Mum feels she missed out a bit on that. I've got a younger sister who's stayed closer to home, and Mum and Dad are involved in quite a lot of decisions in her life – in some ways they are closer to her because of that. Mum would probably be timid about suggesting things or about being involved in or passing judgement on anything that I choose to do.

When I finished my degree, I got married. Thinking back now, Mum and Dad must have been horrified at the thought that I was going to get married at 21. They never said, 'Are you sure?', or 'Don't you think there's a lot of other things that you want to do?' I didn't ever have any resistance from them at all.

I was working by then. Mum and I had talked about that. I enjoyed school work, I was always pretty diligent, and I actually enjoyed varsity. It was always assumed that I would enter the workforce and I don't think Mum and Dad ever saw marriage as a barrier to me doing what I wanted to do. I think they realised that I was fairly clear that I wasn't going to compromise and that marriage was only going to facilitate some of the things that I wanted to do, rather than be a barrier. And that's pretty well what's happened. There are some choices that I've had to make that I mightn't have made if I'd been totally on my own, but by and large there's been nothing that's been a major compromise.

From about my mid-thirties, I started to want to take control of my life a bit more. I felt as if I was a bit directionless. I was enjoying what I was doing, but I suppose it's the puritan ethic in me – I didn't think that there was enough relationship between reward and effort in my work. I just didn't like the old public service environment. I think the new public service environment suits me better in terms of being much more action-orientated and focused.

I went back to university and did an accounting degree and now I probably identify more with my Dad. Accounting was his business, so that's changed our relationship. I don't know whether I've opted for a lifestyle that's more akin to what men do, in terms of being focused on business and career and self-interest and all the rest of it, but I think my father identifies with that more than Mum does.

I've always had a very close relationship with Dad, and more so after I left home. Mum was the one who was always there through our schooling and Dad was a bit more distant, although he was certainly available to us in the weekends. We used to go to the beach and have neat picnics, and Mum and Dad played tennis with us. Mum was always in the tennis club, and could beat me at tennis – nobody else had a Mum who could do that! She's really wonderful, she's lovely, she didn't stop being amazing, but over the years I saw our relationship differently. It might have been the influence of the feminist movement that said, 'Let's just stop and think what we want to do for ourselves and what the choices we want to exercise are.' I think that made me see Mum's life differently and I decided I didn't want the same kind of life. I think for her the feminist movement focused a lot of problems and made her aware of the sort of life that she had found herself in. I think it challenged a lot of what she'd done. Although I don't think she would define herself particularly as feminist and nor do I.

I hope our relationship will change as we get older. I don't intend to work so much. It suits me but it really squeezes out anything else and I don't want to do that, I know that there are other things that I need and want to do. So maybe if I move into a phase when I'm a bit more balanced we will get closer. I've quite often had some anxiety and guilt when Mum's been down to stay and I feel that I haven't been as warm or close as I might. Then she goes and I think if something happens and time's run out, on the evidence of that visit, she wouldn't know that I really loved her. Sometimes I've growled at her or argued with her or challenged something that I know she thinks is important. I feel guilty that I've left her with the feeling that I am argumentative and not very pleasant and I do worry about that. But I've acknowledged and we've talked about how absolutely invaluable she's been in terms of my whole life. I've told her that the reason that I'm able to have what I think is a very satisfying life is the strength and the start that came directly from her, but my life is very different and there is a distance, because I'm a very different sort of person.

The fact that I haven't had children is probably a source of sadness to my folks. I don't have children because I never got around to it – it's never been what I wanted to do next, and now I feel it's getting a bit late. And some of my ambivalence about having kids is a feeling that I had so much from my mother – it was just incredible. I don't want to give as much as she did. I know you don't have to, I know there are options, but I felt that I can't give that to anyone. Mum would never say to me, 'You should have children because I want them.' She sees that I've exercised the sort of choices that she couldn't, and she can on one level identify with that – maybe she would have done the same if she'd been in a different environment.

She got married and had three kids under three straight away, then spent the next 20 years bringing us up. She had other interests and she's probably more creative than I am – she's very involved in the local theatre and produces plays and things – so it wasn't as if she just did nothing, but I just felt that she wished she'd done other things. Although she is supportive of my lifestyle in some ways, I think she thinks that I've gone to the other extreme, that I'm only doing things that suit myself, which is true to some extent. That's what I've chosen to do.

I think I feel more in charge of my life than she was, more able to feel that I can make things happen for myself, or if something's not going the way I want it I can say, 'Okay, what's happening?' I've got options to try something else, whereas I feel Mum's always been much more reactive than proactive and that's what I reacted to in her. Now she says, 'I wish we hadn't lived in the provinces', because she's much more of a city person, she likes the culture and the theatre. But I think she's a bit of a victim – and I was really determined not to be a victim. Mum would redefine that by saying she's got the care and companionship and she's probably got a bigger network of friends who need her than me. Her relationships tend to be based more on dependency, whereas mine are more with friends I interact with. We do need each other from time to time but it's much more of an equal needing – it's different.

Because I was so hellbent on ensuring that I wasn't going to be as self-effacing and self-sacrificing as Mum, I probably worked to build up all sorts of protections and defences against being like that. If I've had a real personal crisis, like relationship problems or serious health matters, I haven't usually told Mum first. I've told her afterwards, after it's been resolved, so the connection is not on a close emotional level. I think she'd like that, but the reality is that I haven't been sharing that sort of thing for 20 years.

Mum and I do share interests, though. She comes down to the Arts Festival, and we both love gardening. The first thing I do when I go home is wander around the garden to see what she's been doing and what she's got in it – that's really neat. And we share a love of nice food and wine and restaurants. It's more like the sorts of things that you would share with friends. She's somebody I like spending time with.

And we certainly have a lot to do with each other. I used to write every couple of weeks when I was overseas and Mum and Dad have still got those letters. It's funny to read them now. I told them lots, but it wasn't personal stuff, it was to do with activities and work. I don't write now at all. I might ring up from time to time and we see each other quite often, every couple of months. We usually see them over Christmas, although a couple of times we've said, 'No, we'll just stay here.' The first time we did that was hard. It was a real signal that we didn't want to be part of the family. But I think after that it was acceptable.

Mum's never done that to me, though. Sometimes I'll just ring up and say, 'Can I pop in?', and I wonder whether she'd ever say, 'It's not convenient.' I don't know that she would. I don't say I would never say to her, 'No, it's not convenient', but I know there's times when I've said, 'No, that's not what I want to do at the moment', but I don't think she would ever do that back to me. It would probably be good for me if she did. I think it would be quite a challenge.

One of the things she's always said – and I don't know whether she's said this in self-defence – is that she doesn't ever want us to do anything out of a sense of obligation, but if we choose not to do something, we know deep down she's probably dreadfully hurt emotionally, though intellectually she says, 'Well, that's your choice.' I know there's been a couple of times when she's wanted me to do something but she's said, 'It's up to you', and I've chosen something different. Perhaps a funeral of a relative whom I don't know particularly.

My brother died in an accident 10 years ago and that affected all of us. I don't think you ever quite get over your kids dying. It affected me in that it focused me on thinking that I really wanted to make sure that I did things for myself. It made me much more hedonistic and goal-directed. Like asking, 'Am I enjoying this job or not?', and if not, saying, 'I don't want to do this because my life could stop tomorrow.' I think it really only served to reinforce all the directions I was moving in anyway. It was very sad and I don't think Mum's ever got over it. It was difficult for her because she became really anxious about me and if I went skiing or tramping or was on the road I could see she was having to really hold back, wanting to say, 'Be careful and ring me up when you get home', because she didn't want to put those anxieties on me.

When I reflect on my relationship with Mum I realise it's been very close and always very good but there was a point in my life when I thought, 'I don't want my life to be like my Mum's.' There are a lot of things about my Mum which I really love but I don't actually want to be available to everybody, so I've had to do things that I know Mum will think are selfish, to forge for myself something that's quite different. In some ways that's been painful because I think we have probably lost the closeness that we had. We don't share the same sort of life space and styles.

Frances

We were brought up during the Depression when things were fairly tough for our family financially. I don't think we appreciated that until later, when we realised some of the things we were forced to do without. Despite the fact that we didn't have much in the way of material things, we had a happy life. We had the most wonderful father – he minded so little of life that he gave everything he could to his children and he never lost his patience. My mother was a little bit inclined to have a short temper, she'd be quite physical, although we probably deserved it anyway.

Both my parents came from fairly humble backgrounds but they both set great store on education. We always had books in the home and we were always helped and encouraged. Without feeling that we were pushed, we felt we were expected to do well and that's probably why we did, although I suppose there was natural ability there too.

I was looked on as an infant prodigy because I was pushed through school at a very rapid rate. I started before I was five but I suspect that was because I was a cheeky nuisance, and they wanted to get rid of me! I finished high school after four years when I was only 15. I was too young to go on to study so I went and worked in a bank, for want of anything better to do, and after three years I started looking around, thinking, 'No, this isn't what I want to do with my life.' My older sister left school and worked in an office, then put herself through university, but there was never any pressure or expectation on us to go. It was something that we had within ourselves. I went off to training college and naturally thought that training college probably wasn't enough, I wanted a degree as well – which I didn't finish because I went overseas. I think it was a lack of stickability as much as anything. But I'm really grateful to my parents for their encouragement and their help with schoolwork and school activities. We tried to do the same with our own children and I tried very hard not to exert any pressure on them at all. They achieved in their own way without that.

I was 18 when I went to teachers' college and still very naive, but not as naive as a lot of people who left straight from school. In fact I felt quite mature compared with them. I boarded at a hostel and that was my first experience of communal living. It came as quite a shock to me really, because in some ways my mother and father still had Victorian attitudes about getting undressed in front of each other, and to go to a hostel where people ran around without any clothes and bathed together so they could have six baths a week instead of three was quite a shock, but I soon adapted.

I wouldn't say I had the best of relationships with my mother while I was growing up. I did a paper for psychology at university in which we had to just write about our relationship with our mums, and when I read mine I was quite surprised at how violent I sounded. I remember saying in it that I thought my father was a much more Christian person than my mother, yet there was nothing un-Christian about my mother. I think it was more that she was a bit short-tempered and not a sympathetic character, but I can see now that it was the pressure of the times and the fact that she was probably wondering how she was going to pay shoe bills for the children and so on. I think it was she who made the decisions in the household and my father would go along with them. In the latter years my relationship with my mother was very close.

At the end of my training college years I didn't want to go back north. The city was where I felt most at home and I just couldn't face going back to being with my mother and father. I thought I'd die of boredom, so I applied for a third year in physical education and went to Dunedin, which was great. It was a way of putting off going back.

At the end of that year I applied for a job in Wellington and worked at a school there for three years. Then suddenly, like a bolt from the blue, I decided I'd like to go overseas, so I started working towards that. I didn't know how I'd pay for my fare. I certainly couldn't get any help from home. I was a reasonably good sewer so I made clothes for the women on the staff and charged them a very modest amount. It didn't take long to save about £75, which was all I needed. I didn't worry about how I'd get home – I thought I would save while I was over there, but of course I didn't.

I was about 24 then. I was away for about 18 months, working in the East End of London. People of my age say there weren't the opportunities, that children today are lucky, but I don't agree, because we were able to travel. We had to do it on our own and it was hard, but if you wanted it badly enough you could. We always hitch-hiked. In those days, it wasn't anything exceptional, but when I look back now I think probably we did take risks. I did some hitch-hiking on my own at times. I look back now and think I wouldn't consider my own children doing that sort of thing.

The funny thing is, my parents never expressed any concern. In retrospect that seems strange to me because I worry when my children go away. I know my father was really quite proud that I was doing this because it was quite unusual, particularly for a Gisborne girl. I remember when I came home I was interviewed by the radio station and he kept this transcript of it, which is quite sweet really.

I came back and worked at an intermediate school before getting married about six months later. I was 25 then, and Bill had been around since I was 16. I didn't have the money to come back, so he paid my fare and everyone said, 'Well, a bargain bride!' I found myself pregnant after about a month. It wasn't what I expected, yet I wasn't upset – somehow you just take such things in your stride. Elizabeth was a joy, she really was – especially after the first few weeks when I really had no idea what to do: she was so tiny I just couldn't handle her with confidence and she was quite unsettled. I didn't know much about babies – well, not many of us do, unless we've got a mother hovering in the background to tell us what we should do. I thought that you had to have a routine and stick to it. If they cried, you just let them cry because it wasn't time to feed them. That was an ignorant thing to do, because the poor little soul was starving and nearly died. I know people think you look back at things through rose-coloured spectacles, but Elizabeth was an absolute paragon. She was bright and quick and it was fun being with her. There was discipline but it was firm but fair. We never had to resort to anything more than just firmness.

She was obviously an intelligent child. She took pride in her school work but was quite a timid girl. She never pushed herself forward. I was a bit worried that she would get trampled on because she was unwilling to assert herself. Then I started to worry that it was our fault because we'd been too dominant. Her school work was very important to her – in fact too much so. I tried to encourage her to go out to school functions and that sort of thing, but she was very happy as she was. It wasn't unusual amongst the people she mixed with and I imagined most children were like Elizabeth. They came home, had a biscuit, went up to their room and did their homework. They perhaps listened to a radio programme, then did a bit more homework or we'd play games and talk. I've found out since that others weren't like that!

It never occurred to me to go back to work. It wasn't until the children were about six, seven and eight that I was approached to do some relieving teaching at their school. And I did a little bit of relieving as a receptionist at a doctor's surgery. I enjoyed it but when it finished I went back to being a mother. I did a few short-term jobs – in the summer time, friends and I used to do a bit of apple picking which didn't require anything except a lot of energy. And about 12 years ago I was involved with people who owned a supermarket – they were going on holiday and asked me if I would manage it. That was really quite an experience. It was very hard work – you had to be on the job by half past seven in the morning to get the bread, and I did the ordering and the cleaning. When they came back they sold the business and bought a delicatessen and I helped them establish it. But on the whole, I've been strangely content with quite a pedestrian life, and it wasn't until the children were well off my hands that I felt I really would quite like something else to do.

Elizabeth left home at 17 to go to university and nobody told me how awful it was going to be. It's terrible, yet no one had ever said, 'You're really going to miss Elizabeth.' I'll never forget coming back from taking her to Wellington, crying most of the way. The same thing happened when she and Mike went to England for the first time in 1976. She would have been 24 then, and they were very airy-fairy about their plans. They said, 'We'll probably be back in a few years.' Of course I thought they may not and I sat at the airport with Bill and had a couple of brandies with the tears pouring down. It was really awful.

When Elizabeth came home after the first term at university I was really nervous. I thought she was going to be different, but she wasn't. It was really great and I think she enjoyed coming home. She'd come in, sit at the snack bar and have about 10 pieces of toast over breakfast while we talked. We didn't have a very intimate relationship but I felt it was comfortable. We used to write every Sunday and I loved Tuesdays when her letter came. The other day I found some letters written when she was at university. They were delightful, but very naive – she wrote about the jersey she wore to lectures that day and how it looked nice with the skirt I made, and so on! We hardly ever write now, we tend to ring.

Within a couple of months of going to university she met Mike and her letters were full of this boy. We liked Mike very much, but I kept thinking of my own life from leaving school to marrying. One tends to think that everyone should have the opportunity to do things. I thought, 'She's marrying at 21' – it seemed young to me. But they were very suited and very happy. We supported them and let them have the sort of wedding they wanted. It was very simple and it got simpler!

They were married in 1974, then went overseas in 1976. We went over the following year and joined them and that was really a very wonderful experience for us, something that we really treasure. I remember going to plays with them and getting on to a tube and tearing across Waterloo Bridge. Great. They expected us to be able to keep up – they still do, although I think perhaps now they're beginning to realise that at 67 I'm not quite as fit as I was!

It may sound a bit strange, but I didn't think about her having children. I'm a fairly philosophical person. I tended to think if they did, that would be their decision. I know there are mothers who are looking for the signs and saying, 'Well, isn't it about time?' And fathers too. But we always thought that was their own choice. There must have been a time quite some years ago when Elizabeth or I brought up the subject, and said she felt their lifestyle didn't really suit having children. Although I think that being a grandparent can somehow round out your life, I don't think now that I would say to Elizabeth, 'Do you regret it or do you wish that things had been different?' Over these last six or seven years her work's become pretty absorbing and very demanding in terms of time and energy so we haven't really had the opportunity to have the talks that we might otherwise have done.

We often say that we miss the sort of relationship that we had a little while ago, but there are times over the last three or four years when she's come up here on business and been on her own, when we've just sat over a bottle of wine by the fire and chatted and I've felt that it's still there. In fact, I know it is. We've had a crisis recently – she came straight away and the warmth between us is as strong as ever.

We share interests but sometimes she makes me feel a little bit inferior so I dither and I know that annoys her, but sometimes I'm nervous with her. Her world is quite foreign to me and quite often I don't really understand what she's talking about. I'll listen but I know that Bill has a better understanding of what she's talking about because it's very technical high-powered stuff and I'm a fairly basic person. She and Bill discuss her work a lot because he feels that he can still contribute something. She often defers to him and is keen to get his opinion on things, which is good.

I don't know what will happen with our relationship, because after we've been together, I sometimes think, she didn't ask what her sister's been doing or what we have been doing. 'What's happening at the theatre? How are so and so?' I put it down to her work that's taken over her life. I hope it's not a deterioration in our relationship, but I honestly don't know. I think it's because over the last few years we haven't seen as much of each other as we used to. Up till five or six years ago they would always come up at Christmas – I didn't want them to feel they *had* to be here for Christmas because we went through the business of having to go to one or other family and the resulting friction between the two families – but their visits are becoming fewer and fewer. We're grateful when they come. I've always said that you really shouldn't expect things of your children, but perhaps in your heart you do. So often you hear, 'They could have done this, they could have done that', but I think that whatever they give back is a bonus.

Although our lives are very different, I think I was past being influenced by the feminist movement. The feminists certainly didn't make me feel that I was a vegetable or a cabbage because I was having to stay home. My house wasn't a prison for me. I did things when I wanted to do them and I felt I had the choice to live the way

I wanted to. I played tennis for many years. That was another interest I had in common with the children. Then I took up golf, and that was something I was able to share with my husband and son. The garden was a big interest too. And for the last 30 years I've been fairly active in our local drama club. I've spent a lot of time on it and I've made it quite an important part of my life. I have now directed plays. That's something I've really enjoyed and I wish I'd started sooner because it's stimulating and rewarding, but, when I'm under pressure to do more, I feel as though perhaps I haven't got the stamina. I sometimes feel the responsibility. I'm only the president, I'm about the only one who doesn't work and therefore I'm the one who's available to do things.

When I look back on my early married days I have pictures of friends coming round with their children and sitting under the tree, with the children playing and us talking recipes. I was a fairly methodical housekeeper. I did things on Monday because it was Monday. In the last 10 to 15 years I've gone to the other extreme. I haven't become grubby and untidy, but I've relaxed any sort of routine and I really enjoy it. I do things on impulse. My husband finds it a bit tedious – he'll come in and say, 'How many things are you doing at once?' But if something occurs to me, I have to go off and do it. I don't think Elizabeth's like that. I think she's more orderly, I don't really know. I felt that when I had children I had to have order in my life. It's the only way I could cope with three small children.

Although I'm not a very positive person, I've still got the feeling that you can do something if you want to, that you can achieve something through sheer willpower. I think that Elizabeth has got that quite strongly.

I think she's got a lot more patience than I have. Elizabeth would probably be more like her father, and he's got more of the qualities my father had. She's inherited her father's flair for organisation. She's a very articulate person and that's something I really envy with her – it's something that's really developed over the last decade. I always get in an absolute panic if I have to give a speech or run a meeting – although people always say I don't give the impression of being in a panic – I never ever say what I thought. I come out with something quite different.

We just accept Elizabeth's work as a fact, and we know that if there is any crisis we can rely on her. There's never any question.

Jean & Mary Anne

This is a story of three generations. Jean's mother was unconventional and colourful, and a powerful if sometimes negative influence on her daughter. It took Jean some time to find her feet and become the confident woman she is now. She married young, then had to invest considerable energy in shielding herself and her daughters from an authoritarian husband and father and the rigours of army life.

In doing this she provided Mary Anne with a model of an independent, capable woman. The relationship between Jean and Mary Anne has always been strong. Although there were times, especially when Mary Anne was moving into adulthood, when they have been at odds, they have moved beyond that to a point where they enjoy each other's support and company. They consider each other their best friend.

Each of them has had to cope with nonconformity and difference, and they have managed to develop as individual people without losing the connection between them.

Jean

I was born in 1931, the fifth of eight children and the first of four children in four years.

Mum delighted me. She was tall, leggy and rather round-shouldered in a twenties sort of way. Mum had style, that's what I liked about her. She wasn't like anybody else's mother. Her clothes looked different, she always had her hair done and she was the only mother I knew who changed every afternoon. If she was up when we went to school – which wasn't very often, because Mum was an evening person – she might wear smart linen overalls and in the afternoon she'd be into a skirt and blouse.

She never had any time. Dad was often off work for years at a time on the invalid's benefit. He was buried in France during the war and suffered from side-effects all his life. Mum wrote a column in the *Evening Post* – 'Over the Fence With Eve' – which brought in 7/6d when it was published. She was always contributing to magazines and papers. She always had a pen and a cigarette in her hand but she was the tidiest smoker I've ever seen in my life.

She was a loving Mum but careless of us too in many ways because she was preoccupied with her own frustrated lifestyle and lack of finance. Even if she had it, she couldn't handle money. Mum was an incurable romantic. She made no positive moves to see (a) that I was educated or (b) that the right opportunity was there. She'd thought I'd rise like baking powder wherever I went. She was right, but it's not the usual way – most parents look out for their children.

When I was six we moved to Mackay's Crossing and my sister and I used to walk to school. One day Dad said it was too wet to go to school but I insisted and on the way I was given a lift in a truck. I had just climbed down when I was knocked over by a car. It was a horrendous accident – I had a double compound fracture of the skull and internal injuries and I was off school a long time. When I went back, the kids who had been my friends were in standard three and I was still in standard one. My whole life was affected. I found it very difficult to learn and had very poor co-ordination, but I still had an imagination that functioned.

A few years after that, Mum found religion. She'd studied all the 'osophies' and God knows what. She was involved with intellectual fringe groups and in my view it was very dangerous because she had a little knowledge. She thought her reading gave her the necessary depth. I've inherited her natural intuition but I don't play around with ideas like she did. As a child I knew it wasn't right; as a young adult I ran from it, and as an adult I just refused to deal with it.

Anyway, Mum was drawn to Catholicism, so we four younger ones were uprooted from the public school in Wanganui where we lived and sent to Holy Infant Convent which was the best thing that could have happened to me because the Sisters were quite liberal. They knew I'd been injured and didn't quite function as the rest did. I took to a religion like a duck to water. I was a spiritual child and I didn't have to answer to anyone or be anyone except God's child!

I didn't have a close relationship with Mum. When I was 11 or 12 I had it in for her. I didn't want to go to Sacred Heart College, I wanted to go to Tech. The Tech girls were switched on – I envied them. They were practical, there was no nonsense about everything being just right. I wanted to be a reporter and learn to write and I knew Tech was the place to go. When I mentioned this I was just about excommunicated – Catholic girls don't go to Tech. I said, 'Why not?'

'What would Sister Monica say? Why would you want to go to Tech, they're rough children?'

I said, 'Because I like them, they do things.' That was the side of Mum I didn't like, because I was right. I would have been a good journalist – I've got an incisive and inquiring mind. But you didn't argue with your parents.

At Sacred Heart I started off in Professional and I couldn't cope. I felt angry at the school, angry with my mother and I was disappointed with myself. I used to go to Virginia Lake by myself at lunchtime because I didn't feel part of it. Eventually I became quite ill with glandular fever and an infection that affected my gums. I had to have my top teeth out and I couldn't face school without teeth – I couldn't face anything without teeth. I was outraged: no one should take teeth out unless it is absolutely essential. The doctor summed it up by saying that I was stifling in the environment at home. I was still at a small school but I just wasn't coping and I was shutting down. And Mum was starting what was to be a prolonged and very bad change of life. The doctor said I had to go away from home. My heart breaks for Mum because mothers get the blame but mothers are victims of their circumstances. How could she be otherwise? She didn't do anything deliberately, it was just the times. I loved her passionately and never, ever doubted her love for me, but it was too much for her – she couldn't ever give me what I wanted, though she did her best.

She decided to send me to Dawson Falls, a mountain resort on Mt Egmont, to recuperate, and Joan Blake, the proprietor, became my mentor. Joan wanted a kitchenmaid but she also wanted special people round her. She took me under her wing – and I stayed for three years. The skills I learned up there consolidated what I had learned at home. It was the best education I could have had.

While I was at Dawson Falls an army recruiting team arrived. The major in charge took a fancy to me and asked me all sorts of questions about my family and so on. Mum was working in Wellington at the time so I told him that, and the next time I was in Wellington, Mum said, 'Oh, I've had lunch with Major So-and-So, he's a lovely man, Jean, you should join the army.' I said, 'What for?' She had the brochure and was all gushy about it – I didn't like Mum one bit at that stage!

I don't know whether she took me or whether I went up to Buckle Street, but I met this man who was really nice. He told me about the programme and I liked the education scheme where I'd be trained as a librarian and in other skills. I saw an opportunity to catch up with formal education. I think I was tested and told to be back in Wellington, then I went back to the Falls and forgot all about it. The Blakes were very annoyed when the local army area officer called to say I had to report in because I was a private in the army. Of course I hadn't said a word, so I left with their anger and not their blessing. By this stage I was glad to go because I had let my friends down. I shied off facing up to my actions – it was another side of my nature which I worked hard to change as I matured.

I went to Wellington and was kitted out. I liked that – I liked the uniform! I learned to drive and type and I was a natural librarian – I grew up in a home that was chock-a-block with books. I was sent to Waiouru to unpack and catalogue books from the Far East and the Pacific region. I was very naive and totally innocent. We were a very pure-minded family – there was no bad language, no drink, we were interested in each other's interests and love affairs but I wasn't prepared for life. I was physically afraid of the dark and afraid of life in many respects. I had a very reserved manner so I wasn't any threat to anybody. Then I met my first husband. He came into the library one night and did what no one else had done – he saluted me. He had twinkly eyes and he read books. Once I met him I could never get away from him, he was always there. He didn't talk much, I did all the talking. He took to dubbing me home on his bike. He never kissed me, he used to shake hands and then salute. After five or six months he said, 'I think we're going together now.' I said, 'You'll have to meet the family.'

He came home and Mum was beside me waiting for him. If Mum liked somebody they were in, even if they were absolute ratbags, but if she didn't, then nobody dared show. Anyway, Mum didn't like him. She said, 'He's not for you, I don't like him. He's going to be bad news.' When we got engaged she summoned me to Wellington and tried to talk me out of it, but by that time I was sweet on my ring and wouldn't give it up.

We were married in Christchurch on 3 February 1951 and my first child was due on 12 February 1952. I had toxaemia almost from conception. I was so sick I had to go home to my parents in Wellington. Mum was loving and kind to me as always, but she took over. It didn't feel like my baby, and my husband was considered a non-event. He could only come up from Christchurch once during the pregnancy and he didn't see the baby till she was eight days old, which was very traumatic. He never really bonded with her. I next saw him when she was five months old and he was going to Korea. He was away two years and came back shell-shocked and battle-weary. I had no idea of what to expect from him. From being on active duty to domesticity with a wife and a small child within 24 hours – I ask you! Everything got on his nerves and after four days he went home to his mother and the peace of the family home.

Mum thought we had finally finished and she was happy as a lark. Home was open to me and Helen, but I was actually seeing my husband. There was nowhere to live because housing in New Zealand was at a premium, and we finally got together when Helen was three and a half. We had to live in a camping ground to start with, then moved from house to house. He was a different man after Korea. There was no counselling, he drank a lot and I didn't know how to handle it. I prayed a lot and that annoyed him, so we were on a collision course.

I had three miscarriages after Helen but eventually became pregnant with Mary Anne. It was a difficult birth, a big drama, but when I came to, there was a big lump in the bassinet and I can't tell you the enormous joy I felt. I could hardly speak. The matron tipped the bassinet up and I looked at Mary Anne and couldn't believe it because here was a mass of hair and a rosy big fat baby. She looked in that moment exactly like my mother when she was young and yet like her paternal grandmother. I looked at her, she looked at me and I said, 'Well, hello cheeky,' and that's how it's been.

Mary Anne is multi-talented – she'll hate me saying that but she is – and my girls had to have what I hadn't had. First of all, assurance that I wouldn't let them make decisions that they weren't able to make. I didn't care what they thought of me, I was their mother. I ruled the roost. It was our house and they would go to school, they would do this, they would do that. I did everything I could within our means to make sure their lives were like everybody else's. They had the proper lunches, the right shoes, whatever. They also knew that I was in charge. At the same time I didn't stifle them – they had plenty of books. They didn't have all that I wanted for them, but they had the best that I could provide.

I knew one day I would leave my husband, but until they were grown up I decided I would take whatever came my way with interludes out. To my mind it was important they had both their parents, because no matter how harsh he seemed he was their father and he did love them. He had skills I didn't have and he was a good provider. I didn't have enough confidence or ability to earn the money to see that they had what was required. I had been deprived myself and that was not to be for them. So no matter how erratic it was, I was doing my best.

In the meantime, I was annoying my mother. She didn't think anyone should have to put up with what I put up with, so I was pulled between my husband and Mum. They were coolly correct with each other for years. Finally there came a point where I couldn't go home any more. The welcome mat was off the doorstep because I always ran back to my husband and the stressful life.

When Mary Anne was about five, I left him for nearly two years. I was terrified of life outside marriage and went through some very, very hard times, but eventually developed a good lifestyle. I had a contract arranging flowers in hotels and buying and selling flowers and I wanted to buy a house. The town clerk's job was going where I lived and my husband could have applied for the job with his background. We weighed up the pros and cons because we were always very honest with each other and it came to several columns in favour of us being together and having a normal life. Against that was one sentence – 'I love the army' – so I gave it all up and went back with him to the army.

When Vietnam developed, he was commissioned and we went to Papakura. I came into my own there. It was a small camp, I liked the other women and we were close. For the first time I had a niche. Then he went off to Vietnam. That was the end of my husband and the beginning of terrible trauma for me which only ended recently. I was once again mother and father to the girls, a solo parent in a marriage, which I was very annoyed about.

When he came back from Vietnam he was a very sick man and Mary Anne lost her greatest pal. His deterioration was hidden from the world but it was diabolical for us living with it, so I sent Mary Anne away. I made a great mistake sending her back to my old school. I should have let her go to the local college because in spite of everything she would have done well, but that didn't seem the thing to do at the time.

My husband was finally medically released from the army and his pay stopped, so Mary Anne had to come home. We went back to the farm and used his savings to buy nurse cows and so on. The army don't tell you what help's available and we had no advice, no help. Mary Anne should never have had a broken education. She went to the local district high school and they ganged up on her because she was the daughter of the toffee-nosed bastard on the hill. She never let on.

When she missed her School Certificate, her father tore all the posters off the wall of her bedroom, then threw everything out – he said she'd idled her time away at school and made no allowances for anything. I lost my cool, I couldn't bear it because she didn't deserve it. I redid her room and she did School C again, but she wouldn't go on. She should have – she could have been extremely good at academic work.

Her first job was at a big oil company. They were very keen on her and wanted to send her to Adelaide but she was also very keen on nursing. She reckoned we forced her into it – we have totally different memories of this. She did get into nursing and since then she has done a whole range of things.

The differences between Mum's life and mine and between my life and Mary Anne's have been enormous. Mum was born in 1901 when her mother was 46 years old. All her life her mother was a little old lady dressed in either black or navy blue. Mum was exceptionally bright and a scholarship winner but she grew up like Topsy. She was also a runaway romantic bride at 17, had two children before she was 21, and six more later. An omnivorous reader, she wrote all her life but I don't think it ever occurred to her to make a career from writing. She was a prisoner of her time. As the mother of a large family she was stuck with that state.

One of the so-called 'selfish generation', I was born in 1931, during the Great Depression. I was fortunate to be born a middle child because I had others to learn from but also learned to be responsible for the younger children. Marrying at the age of just 20 was the silliest thing I ever did because my level of awareness was practically zero. But unlike my mother, I wasn't trapped by the unbreakable bonds of a large family and her unresolved personal and emotional conflicts. Although I loathed the frequent upheavals and constantly trying to belong, my marriage did provide me with a highly developed inner resource. I learned to become self-reliant and to have the courage of my own convictions. Over the years I have become sure and strong. I've worked to overcome every trait that would have made me fail or condemned me to the kind of life Mum had.

Mum catered for our minds but she wanted to know everything that was going on and it really wasn't her right. It took me years to shake off the probing and the intrusion. She was also a pacifist and wouldn't let us be aggressive or fight, which put us at a very serious disadvantage in the competitive sense. We weren't prepared for argumentative people or children who could stand up for their rights. When I began in business I had to really assess how I was going to cope with that. I then realised that we had been conditioned not to defend ourselves and it wasn't enough to say a prayer and hope it would be all right. And I had to do things over and above what ordinary women did in those days, like get out and earn.

When we went to South Africa after my second marriage I was relieved to get away from her, not because I didn't love her, but because she took too much out of my life. She was a great mother but an interfering, emotional mess. They were the two sides of her. I respect and revere her and admire her courage but my heart breaks for the things she couldn't overcome. She didn't knuckle down to a discipline, and that frightened me. I've been tough with my girls. There were certain things they jolly well had to do. I tried as much as possible to give them freedom but to keep them within the discipline.

Mary Anne's life has been different. She could have been a ballet dancer, she's an artist, she's extremely musical, she writes excellent stories. She's also a Taurean so she has all her father's provider and home traits as well. She was a courageous child, she had the H-Bug, eczema, asthma – we nearly lost her three times. Her courage and spirit have been one of the greatest things in my life. Yet she was a cheeky, mischievous, naughty little monkey. She bullied Helen and me yet she has a sensitivity that is still childlike.

She heeded our advice to 'do your growing up before you marry, *don't* marry too young.' She was nearly 30 when she married and in my view she is living her life in the right order. Our home discipline may have been too harsh for too long, but she has achieved all the skills that educate and broaden the mind. She has been educated, trained, retrained, travelled extensively, had diverse work experience and is still learning and growing. She became a mother and is developing parenting skills. Mary Anne is of today's world – she is prepared for today and tomorrow. In turn, she is preparing her son for his time.

I'm very proud of Mary Anne – she's irritated me, driven me nuts, she's done her own thing, she's her own woman, but she has every right to be. Whatever she does, I don't give a damn, because Mary Anne is one of life's true people. She's highly creative, she's extremely compassionate, she's totally family-minded and yet she's a free spirit. She's very much like my mother. She has an intellectual bent and she's a night person, like Mum. She has no time sense either, and nor did Mum, but when you least expect it she turns up on time. I love Mary Anne and my friendship with her is over and above our relationship. It's the same with Helen. They are my best friends on earth. I can fight with them and now and again they go too far and I jump. I don't owe Mary Anne anything. She had the best of me and she's seen pretty well the worst of me but she's also saved my life; she's seen me through a lot because she is never far behind me. Wherever I've gone, sooner or later she turns up. I don't care what she does, with whom or where – she's all right by me.

At 35 she is assured, reliable and full of potential. At 60 I am confident my girls are equipped for their time. My grandchildren are fortunate, their lives will never be as bleak as mine and my mother's. But overall, all things are relative. We can only do our best as we see it and know it. 'To thine own self be true' will always be the main criterion of successful survival.

Mary Anne

I was born in 1956, a frail child, very small for my age, who caused Mum constant worry with numerous hospital visits and near death experiences. I still feel personally insecure at times and I think part of it stems from being left alone in hospital as a child. Mum was the epitome of a warm mother – always warm and physically loving but not a good cook! She was tall, very pretty and feminine. She loved music, the arts and books, and encouraged us to read and write stories. When I was five she took us to see the Royal Australian Ballet perform 'Swan Lake', after which I developed a life-long passion for ballet. I didn't realise at the time that she actually had to sell things so we could go.

She always had our home full of flowers and paintings. She was a connoisseur of good classical music – Schumann and Chopin that you didn't hear usually – and we always had a piano and lovely china, so no matter how grotty or plain our surroundings were, Mum always made them special. She tried to expose us to her own family as much as possible although Dad never really approved. Her family was outrageously dramatic and undisciplined, full of colour and freedom and warmth. I think it helped us to keep some link with normality: growing up in military camps can be very dehumanising.

Mum and Dad separated for two years when I was five and we lived with my grandparents in a huge sprawling mansion. It was a magic house in a magic time. Mum began her first business there in 1962, growing flowers for the Palmerston North market – gladioli, carnations and copper beech. I was very happy there. I had my grandparents nearby, a grass tennis court, a huge orchard with granny smith apples, a rose garden and a swing bridge over the creek at the back. Mum's health improved there and Dad calmed down a bit. But it was back to reality when they reunited. I loved my father as much as my mother and I remember feeling really sad thinking of Dad on his own without us.

The army dominated our lives and Mum served as a buffer and a softener between the army, Dad and us. He was totally authoritarian, the white gloves checking the dust. He used to give us our pocket money on a Saturday, but only after our jobs were inspected. Every now and then we wanted a pay rise and we used to have to write to the Arbitration Court, which was him. He'd sit for, say, two weeks, then he would send a letter back from the Arbitration Court granting us a pay rise with back pay – three shillings' back pay and we were rich. Yes, it was very tough, very different.

I went to about seven primary schools. I was bright but I always felt shy inside. I had to learn to make friends straight away or I had no one because we moved so often.

By the time I was 10 we lived in Papakura. It was the happiest and most stable time I can remember as a child. Mum always let me go and do my own thing, but I never got into trouble and times were not as dangerous then. Kids used to make their own adventures and we had a whole military camp to do it in. Mum was a devout Catholic, so we were as well, and I used to quite enjoy going to church, dressing up and looking at people and wearing mantillas. I felt I had a supreme power because I was a Catholic and would always make it to heaven. I had a lot to learn!

I remember Mum used to get sick periodically, probably every six to eight weeks. It was a mixture of physical, mental and emotional strain. When she ran off the rails it usually meant three or four days in bed, sometimes a week if it was really bad, and if Dad was there it was terrible. He ruled with an iron fist and nothing ever happened in our lives until she was on deck again. She was our protector and friend.

Mum was an involved, organised and intelligent woman and I liked that, but I also became her worst and greatest critic around then and I still am. Mum and I are very alike but I have my father's harsh realistic streak which gives me the ability to sum her up and perhaps identify her problems – especially as I get older. She used to get angry when I criticised her, which I can understand because she was only in her mid-thirties then, the same as I am now. It would aggravate me if I had a daughter doing that, but I wouldn't be as gentle or as understanding as she was. She is really patient, something which I'm not.

Then early one Tuesday morning Dad left for Vietnam by helicopter, two hours after his mother had died. Once again Mum took on the role of the double parent which she played all through our lives. When he came back 15 months later, our lives changed hugely. He had what they called 'Saigon Bug', but it was Agent Orange and he was severely chemically poisoned. He was a psychotic wreck and displayed really disturbed behaviour. For example, when he left he was highly conservative, and when he returned after living with the Americans for so long he had to have 'pop' music blaring all the time. It was very strange.

I was sent to boarding school, to Mum's old convent, but Mum had painted a far prettier picture of it than it actually was – rose-coloured glasses has Mum. I was very, very homesick. I felt ill because I missed Mum so much. The nuns were diabolical. We had to go to church every day, Benediction twice a week, awful food except on All Saints' Day and St Joseph's Day, and very tough discipline – but not as tough as Dad. I'd gone from one severely disciplined environment into another archaically disciplined environment. I became fat because I used to fill up on bread and anything else I could lay my hands on. I wrote to everybody – my grandmother, my aunts, my sister in Auckland – to send me food, so I had about three or four food parcels coming every fortnight and money for the tuck shop.

I became very naughty and by the second week I was already banned to the kitchens on Sundays to do the dishes. It was dreadful. I did the dishes all year. I went off religion, didn't like it or respect it at all. I used to write three letters a day home saying, 'Take me away from this place.' It was an obsession. Mum used to fear the mailman and he felt sorry for Mum. She thought I was exaggerating, of course.

Meantime Dad was deteriorating rapidly and she was shielding us from the problems that would emerge later. We didn't know how sick he was or how serious the situation was, but when I was in the fourth form Dad was medically released from the army. In those days there was no Accident Compensation or golden handshake or anything like that – they had their savings and that was it. It's sad because he'd done so much and worked so hard, and so had Mum, but there was nothing, and that's not so long ago.

Mum took him back to his family farm to die and I never knew how desperate things were. She used all their savings to get the main house up to a liveable standard, organised for the weeds and gorse to be removed and had fences and gates put in because the place was just a wreck. And eventually when I came home from school they were so poor I couldn't go back, which was rather wonderful. I had to finish my secondary education at a rough co-educational school in a freezing works town. I went from a select eccentric environment to a rough one where the Maori girls immediately ganged up on me and wanted to beat me up because they didn't like the way I spoke. They asked, 'Are you English?'

So at 15 I learned to talk my way out of bad situations. The other girls thought I was spoilt because we had a new car, which a lot of people didn't have, and Mum was slim and attractive. She was threatening to them and Dad was so sick he was totally aloof, so it wasn't like we fitted in. But I went all out and once again used my personality and my ability to make friends and overcame a lot. Those times were gloomy and dark, unhappy. We were very poor but I never really knew that, I just knew things were tough. It was the demise of their marriage and there were regular arguments – Dad with his heavy military shouting and bossing. I used to quake in my room and feel sorry for Mum and yet at the same time I felt angry that she couldn't be as verbally violent as I am against Dad. I'm worse than he is at times. And I could never give her my support because it put me in the line of fire.

It was a tough time then. I used to watch Mum get up early, cook breakfast and organise me and Dad and the animals, drive 50 kilometres to town, work a full day innovating a whole new business style, drive home, cook dinner, tidy up and basically carry the lot, and cope with Dad drinking heavily and being abusive and critical. I didn't drink alcohol for years after that. I admired her but I felt very sorry for her. I felt sorry for Dad as well because I loved him so intently. She had no moral support from anyone, none at all. She worked like a Trojan to re-establish first us and then Dad into a normal life, because he did get better. She always compromised, which I think is the by-product of being a woman. I remember Dad screaming at her, 'Compromise, there is no such word as compromise.' And I thought that summed up what she was up against.

When I was about 17 the wheels were starting to turn for Mum. She was becoming very successful in her business and she organised me my first job with a thriving oil company as an office junior. I could have taken it a lot further but their marriage was on the rocks, they needed me to be in a safe environment, and where safer than a nurses' home? So I went nursing. I was emotionally very immature, still very much the child, so I agreed to go, but it was the worst possible career choice for me because I'd had the discipline at home, the discipline of school and now the still very old-fashioned discipline of nursing, and I'd had a gutsful before I even started.

The world had really changed by then. It was 1974: Deep Purple, Black Sabbath, heavy rock music, Buddha sticks soaked in opium oil, country garden perfumes and cheesecloth dresses – I launched into all of this stuff. I had no idea about sex or boys but at 17 I had my first joint. I told Mum the next day because she's the sort of mother I could tell, and she just about drove off the road. She knew nothing about drugs and she knew nothing about venereal disease – not that I ever got that. She was very naive, very innocent. What she did know she would tell us and I always felt that she couldn't tell me enough because she didn't know enough: I guess that's the plight of all children.

So as a young, naive, immature girl coming from a broken home, I really launched into this new era. I became a total hedonist! Jobs were a dime a dozen. All we wanted was to travel, listen to music and have a good time. Basically that was it. It was no big deal if you didn't have UE or go to university, but that's where I actually wanted to go. I probably would have done really well because I needed that freedom on campus instead of the uptight, matriarchal nursing system.

Meanwhile Mum was a successful person and a much-sought-after celebrity in our small regional centre, involved in politics, always on the radio and in the newspaper. She was well off and she had a beautiful home and a flash car. She'd separated gently from Dad by taking a flat in town and going home at weekends and then gradually the weekends tapered off. She had men who fancied her and I was really pleased for her but I used the situation for myself. Because she had it all, it was easy for me just to storm in and get my way and storm out again. I was very immature. She was pushing me away and I felt hurt and angry and rejected, yet she had to do that because she needed her space.

When she left Dad she took nothing from the farm except her own personal items – she left all her paintings and furniture and stuff, which was an extremely good example for me. She didn't want the home to be broken up, so that there would always be somewhere for us to go and she didn't want Dad to have to sell the farm in order to pay her out. By doing that she has ensured that we have a family farm to go to for the rest of our lives. She's a really selfless person.

I quite enjoyed nursing and I was a good nurse but I rebelled terribly and just scraped through every step of the way. After nearly five years in the job I woke up one morning and thought, 'Is this it? Is this all there is?' I was 22 and I felt that my fate was sealed – if I was lucky I would marry a house surgeon and settle down and have kids. I knew that my life could never be that simple. I think now my first step towards self-realisation was to move to Wellington and start a completely new life.

During this time, Mum had met and married her second husband. I liked him – he told me he loved her and that was enough for me. They were living in Wellington and I moved in with them for a while, which was a nightmare. We had grown so far apart we couldn't stand each other, which I think is a very natural process. Then she and Steve decided to move to South Africa. That was the ultimate cut-off and I thought, 'Right, you obviously aren't interested in me. Go to South Africa.' This was about 1978 and the anti-apartheid movement was really heating up. I was ignorant of South Africa but anti it nonetheless. And of course I was back in the same situation as I was when Dad was in Vietnam. I couldn't really say where my mother lived or, later on, that I was going to live there, because it was very uncool. People wouldn't talk to me at parties when they knew I was going to go and live in South Africa.

When Mum moved, my life changed. I started to grow up pretty fast and we didn't really communicate for a couple of years – in fact, I loathed her. But I missed her too. I'd go out on my own to lunch and see a mother and daughter lunching. I'd feel lonely and empty and envious that I couldn't have the joy of going out with a mother to do a bit of shopping or whatever. We were the furtherest apart we have ever been physically and emotionally. I felt completely misunderstood by her. I felt she wouldn't trust me, that she wouldn't see me as a credible adult, able to cope responsibly with most things. I may have resented her going away and leaving me but it never surfaced as an issue between us. I have never felt jealous of her success, only thrilled for her.

I had my first real relationship in Wellington which went very wrong and all but destroyed me and that's when Mum phoned me and said, 'You're coming to South Africa.' She made sure I did because I felt suicidal after losing this fellow and she bailed me out financially, as she's always done. I really had no choice. My family over-ruled me and between them organised me into a tin hat. They're like that where I'm concerned – they all know what's best for me and become a lean, mean fighting-machine when my happiness is at stake! I have great need of that. Having a departure date and a fully paid ticket didn't make me want to go or even want to be close to Mum again, but I knew I had very limited options at that stage and it was the perfect 'out' from my heartbreak and poverty. When I arrived I was as prickly as a hedgehog and didn't like her at all. I didn't respect a single thing that she was doing and didn't understand. All I could say was, 'Oh yes, but Soweto's not electrified, you know. What about the poor blacks?' and all this. I came in on a wrong tack really, but she was very kind and gentle and gave me a lot of space and freedom – and a job and a car. She set me up.

I'd only been in South Africa for three weeks when I was out and about searching for the black music clubs, which is where I met my husband. I still found it very hard to cope with Mum because she was riding a very high wave but after a couple of years I could start to see through some of the people that she was dealing with and I knew she was going to come a cropper. I gave her some very sound advice which she wouldn't listen to and that was when we started to truly interact. She was just 50, so I guess she was entering a new phase as well. She was let down really badly by these people and came back to New Zealand for a holiday.

When she returned, I don't know what had happened but I changed. I loved her. We had so much to talk about. She brought with her that feeling of New Zealand I desperately needed, and we were able to bridge the gap by being New Zealanders first. Then came the time where my strengths outweighed hers and I became her protector in a way, not physically like she used to be to me, but emotionally – I became her friend and the one person in the world other than Steve whom she could really trust. She could say anything and it didn't shock me and that's really how our relationship has developed.

I'm very like my mother and perhaps the older I get the more I realise it. We both have very strong appreciations of life and other people, art, colour, music and whatever, although we differ in our tastes. Emotionally we're similar. Mum and my husband are the only two people I can have a really blazing row with and end up still talking, and feeling far better about things, even if I was wrong.

I like to talk to her every day just to keep in touch. We don't *have* to do that, because when we're both busy we can go four or five days and not speak, but when we're both at a low ebb or in need it's good for us to talk to each other every day. But she never over-involves herself with my life and friends and she can see me clearly when I am out of sorts with myself. She has been consistently kind to me too, which I need at certain times.

Our lives have been completely different but we have both had to overcome ignorance and being different. We are both friendly, open and giving in our natures with no hidden agendas. Over the years we have encountered people who have been suspicious or jealous of our natural friendliness and tried to use or abuse us. I learned in my late twenties not to 'give' of myself to such a degree. Mum learned this, I feel, in her late fifties. We both collapse emotionally in the same way but I take criticism and advice more readily than she does. I suppose that has a lot to do with having had more education and formal training. We both despise greed and money-grabbing people. We're both very politically aware and hold strong views and I believe we're both true socialists really. I didn't realise how much of a socialist I actually am until this year, despite the conservative right-wing values which were instilled over the years. I have a natural and quite intense interest in the process of politics and in this respect I am similar to Mum. The difference is that she became a 'politician'. I prefer a background involvement because I know where the real power lies and I'm quite wary of some of the people involved in party politics and find the narrowness and loyalty to the process quite alien to my sort of approach.

I'm still Mum's hardest critic. I say the hard things that she has to hear and she's still learning to trust what I say. Similarly, she can say things to me and I will listen. If your mother or your daughter won't say those things, who will?

Gwitha & Lowana

Gwitha and Lowana's story is one of repeating patterns. It is also a story which illustrates quite poignantly the effect of social policy on women's ability to care for themselves and their children.

Both women had children without a live-in partner. Gwitha gave birth to Lowana in Auckland and raised her alone, without the support of her family, at least in the early years, and without the aid of the Domestic Purposes Benefit. She had to work hard to keep herself and her child but never lost her faith in people or her generosity of spirit. When Lowana became pregnant at 17, Gwitha supported her in giving up the baby for adoption, knowing how hard it was to manage alone. Lowana did so, but a few years later became pregnant again and kept the baby, raising him with the help of a benefit.

Both women tell their story with quiet understatement, playing down both the difficulties they faced and their own strength. Unlike many stories of this kind, theirs has a happy ending which continues to delight me.

Gwitha

I was born in a small Hawke's Bay town and had a really good childhood. Mum and Dad always encouraged us to do well at school but they didn't pressure us. They were more inclined to build up a good character and good work attitudes. We never heard gossip at home. We were never allowed to talk about people with handicaps or anything like that – we had to accept them – so there were always these subtle quiet influences.

I didn't learn much about the facts of life, of course, though we were aware that men got away with it and girls didn't. We didn't really know the emotional areas, so I was idealistic. I didn't have a clue about the power of my own sexuality. I was spiritually inclined and when I was in my teens I wanted to be a medical missionary. Well, I made a few wrong choices in life and didn't do that.

I went nursing but didn't finish my training. I got engaged to a boy who was going overseas as an accountant for a mission. When he'd been away a while he wrote to say he was interested in someone else. That was a bit devastating. I ran away from facing everybody at home and went up to Auckland. I didn't manage my feelings very well and got caught up with Lowana's father. I was in a state where I could succumb to my weaker side and I did. There were no easily available contraceptives then, so that was how it came to be. I didn't know what to do. I remember taking an overdose of the medication I had for a thyroid condition, but fortunately the desire to die wasn't strong enough and I lived. But I'm glad I did it in some ways because it gives me an understanding of the stupid things we can do when we are emotionally disturbed.

I went back home and didn't say anything to my mother at the time. When I finally told my parents I was pregnant, they reacted badly because the father was a Tongan. We were never brought up with racial prejudice, but when it came to marriage or having a baby, Mum discovered that she didn't like it. Dad just put his arms around me and said, 'You're having a bad time, kid', and that was it.

I had a friend I'd been nursing with who had a baby and I talked to her. She was amazed because I was always regarded as a good girl, but she told me about St Mary's in Auckland and I went there. It was a home that took both married and unmarried women. The unmarried girls' part wasn't exactly like a prison, but it was strictly secret. You could go there and have your baby and nobody need know. They had this particular belief that it wasn't the baby's fault and the rule was that you had to give him six months of your life, breastfeeding if it was physically possible and looking after him. There was a sickness benefit which went to the home and they took care of all our medical needs. We were secluded and wore smocks – it was a very strict regime – but there was care and concern and we did have some fun.

When I went there I thought I would adopt Lowana out – I would adopt her and then go home and that would be that. But of course I was older – 24 – and once I had her and started feeding her, I thought, 'No, I'm going to keep her.' By that time, too, I had got my spiritual life right – I felt I had sinned against God and society, but I experienced forgiveness. If I didn't have my faith, my life would have been very different.

After the six months was up, my father said, 'You can't come home.' I've never held that against him because I understood why he did it. I was a local girl, I had nursed locally, I was well known, I was liked. I think it wasn't so much that he couldn't cope with the shame of it, as that he didn't want me to be thought less of, and if I wasn't there people would go on thinking it was all right. However, my mother managed to come and see me when I was in one of my housekeeping jobs when Lowana was about a year old. It was seven years before I went home.

In the meantime I was doing housekeeping jobs which weren't so bad and some domestic work which wasn't very nice, although I made good friends with some of my employers. When Lowana was about three, her father said he'd look after her so she went back to Tonga with him. I went over about six months later, stayed for about six months and decided to bring her back. It had on my passport, and on her birth certificate, that she was illegitimate – it was before the new law came in where you could get a certificate without giving it away. I went to see the solicitor who handled our affairs when we were in the home. He suggested that I adopt her, so I actually adopted Lowana, legally. And from then on until we became completely open about it, I would say, 'This is my daughter, Lowana, I adopted her when she was seven.' I told the people who really mattered the true story but the adoption was also the truth, and it covered her, it covered Mum and Dad, and it covered me.

She came back to New Zealand when she was six and didn't remember me – she had a few difficulties, one being that she didn't speak English. At that time I was working as a nurse aide at the Sunrise Home for Blind Children. They valued my work and when I told the matron about Lowana, she went to the man in charge and Lowana came and stayed with me. Then we found that the hours were difficult with her going to school, so I got a job as the cook, because the cook was off duty between two and three and I could meet her after school and send her off in the mornings. We lived like that for a wee while and then I cracked up, I had a bit of an emotional breakdown.

After that I was offered a job as co-matron with a friend of mine at the Sunrise Home, but what to do with Lowana was a problem. I decided God must be looking after me: I was visiting an aunt and saw in her church paper an advertisement for the Friends School in Wanganui. I rang them and Lowana was able to go to that school, which meant I could take the job. I felt that I wouldn't do justice to her or the job if I had her, yet I really wanted to do the job *and* I wanted to look after Lowana.

It was a co-educational boarding school with a married couple in charge, and I thought, 'Good, she's going to get "brothers" and a father figure there.' The first year she felt that I had rejected her; after that it was all right and she stayed there for the rest of her primary school years.

One of the things that motivated me when I was getting work was what I owed society, because although we didn't have the DPB, we had free medical care and the family benefit. It wasn't very much but I was grateful for what we got back from our taxes and of course it took me a while to work the sense of sinning against society out of my system. I was determined that my daughter was not going to be classed as a snotty-nosed illegitimate, so she was always dressed very nicely. She never had a runny nose. And I was determined that she'd have a good education because she was quite a clever kid.

I can remember my doctor saying, 'Now you must never, never tell Lowana she's your own, she must always think she's adopted', because even then, 10 or 12 years later, it was still a very immoral thing and he thought it wasn't good for her to think that her mother was immoral. But I knew that God had forgiven me and I had so many wonderful friends I just knew that it was wrong *not* to tell. So while she was still at Friends School we had a mother and daughter heart-to-heart talk and I told her. She was so pleased that I kept her and knew that I loved her. That's how she saw it, because that's how it was, so we didn't have any difficulty that way.

We met difficulties later. I'd always said that I could never expect my daughter to make a confidante of me but when you're growing up you do things and think things which aren't always quite what you'd like your mother to know about, because you always think your mother never thought those things and you don't want to talk about them.

She didn't have a father, I didn't have a car, so when she went out with her friends I had to trust that she was behaving herself. Sometimes she wouldn't come home until late but she would ring up and say, 'Oh, I'm at so-and-so.' It didn't matter where she was, she always rang me, but she didn't always tell me what she was doing. I'd imagine all sorts of things, like she was beaten up, or dead or raped or something. She did get herself into strife but she was a good girl apart from that. She never ever showed any anger or resentment.

Lowana was clever enough to go to university but she didn't go. I was like my parents – I would have liked her to have done something with her brains but I was more concerned about her character. I still don't know whether I made a mistake in making her stay at school. She resented it. I wanted her to do well in the sense that I didn't want her to waste her life, and I feel that if we've been given brains it's got nothing to do with us, it's a gift from God and we have a responsibility to use them to help mankind. Sounds a bit idealistic, but that's how I felt.

She got School Cert and Sixth Form Certificate then went into psychopedic nursing but didn't finish. Like me she started several jobs but didn't follow through. I could never say anything to her because I never completed anything either, but when I became matron of Sunrise Home I realised that every job I had had – whether domestic work or housekeeping or office work or nursing – had contributed. I'd lived a life that was pretty tough for those nine months at St Mary's and I understood the grief of parents parting with their children. Though I hadn't had formal training, everything that I'd done fitted me to cope with those kids and their parents, particularly the mothers. So I couldn't get too het up when Lowana didn't finish things. I couldn't say, 'Well dear, you know I didn't finish anything and look what a mess I'm in', because I was in a good job at the time.

She was 17 when she left home. We were sharing a room, which would have been about the same area as this whole flat. Lowana had her bed and bits and pieces down one end and I had mine at the other. She couldn't join in with a lot of the housework because the nurses were doing that sort of thing and the cook was doing the cooking, but she was never allowed to go out on a Saturday morning until she cleaned our bathroom. She said to me later, 'I hated it at the time, Mum, and I hated you for doing it but I was grateful when I went flatting because I could cope with the bathroom.'

She had a little girl when she was 17 and had her adopted. For quite a while I felt almost guilty, not guilty really, but distressed, because I wasn't in a position to help her keep her. I had been able to keep my child and she couldn't. I couldn't take the child and bring it up myself because I was working. I didn't have enough money to leave work and buy a little house and look after the baby. It was fairly traumatic for both of us. I felt I had failed her because we had talked very frankly about these things and she knew the kind of life she'd had to lead because I wasn't married. I did feel sad that I hadn't been able to protect her enough from that. But at the same time she was still a person in her own right. She had her weaknesses, she had had her rejections, her unhappiness, her everything, so I had to accept what she did. I didn't feel disgraced or anything like that and I suppose I secretly felt glad that society was more accepting and would make it easier for her.

We were able to talk about her pregnancy and I got her into Bethany. I felt bad about that too, but we talked about it and I let it be her choice because I had no right to influence her one way or the other – it had to be her decision. I just supported her in that.

Then, when she was in her early twenties she had another baby. It was quite deliberate. She rang me up and told me she was pregnant and said she was going to keep him. I remember thinking, 'Good heavens, she ought to know better', but at the same time I realised what it was. She had never been able to really share with me the effect of the adoption. I knew it made her sad, but I hadn't really realised just how much until recently. I didn't adopt *her* out – I would have understood if I had. When she had the baby it was becoming known that a lot of girls who had adopted their babies quite often had another one because it is the only way they could cope with the grief – it wasn't a result of sexual promiscuity, it was the grief.

I would have liked her and the baby's father to get married then, but I've never been one to believe in marriage as a solution. If they really love one another and are mature enough to cope, good. But not just for the baby.

In the meantime I had given up working with the blind. I had what was like a halfway home – kids who had been in trouble came and lived with me. I was like a Mum to them. It was a big house and Louana was able to live in the flat downstairs. Later, when the baby was about six, his father came back from overseas and he and Louana fell in love again and got married! That was a happy occasion for me because I felt that Louana was no longer having to work and struggle to bring up her son. I think I'm a romantic at heart. Her son had a father, and boys need fathers even more than girls. Well, I don't know if they really do but one thinks they do – they certainly need a stronger hand at times.

Since she married we've grown a lot lot closer. When they married they had nothing. They were living in Auckland, and had three more children quite close together. Then they decided to move to Hawke's Bay because there were better opportunities there. Her husband came down in the March and I came at the end of

June. Lowana came down a month later. She was pregnant with her fourth child when she came down and I stayed with them for about 12 months, helping them – by that time I'd completely retired so it was okay.

When they first got married Lowana used to help her husband a bit, but she didn't go out to work. With the last two babies she had post-natal depression and reached a stage where she thought she was a complete and utter failure as a wife and mother. Of course she wasn't, but she felt she was. Through a series of circumstances she decided she'd do a job, which really gave her a lift because she found that even after having all those children and all the harassments she could still use her brain and was a person in her own right.

I used to get really cross when people said to me, 'And what is Lowana doing? Where is she working?' I'd say, 'She's at home', and they'd say, 'Oh.' To me, five children and a husband was a full-time job. I think a lot of them thought that I should be looking after the children, because a lot of grandmas do. Of course I do a lot of babysitting for them and I did look after her eldest child at one stage when she had a job, but it has always been a clear understanding between us that I am not a built-in babysitter. She's never taken me for granted. It's been an issue between a few mothers and daughters about how far that grandmothering role should extend. It's a tricky one, and I'm just blessed to have a daughter who, even though she's needed me, has never taken advantage of it. People on the outside might think so, but that's because people think in stereotype ways. I know what she hasn't asked me to do, I know what pressure she hasn't put on me.

When Lowana was not working people used to be disapproving because that was the period when everybody ought to work. It was a swing-over from when I was young when it was, 'You shouldn't be working, you ought to be at home', and now to be a mother is the lowest. Where did that come from? I reckon that a mother needs the most skill of any person in any job because she has to able to do so many things for so many people with different temperaments, and other people can only do one thing at a time. I think if I ever crusade about anything it would be to work to prove that women at home are as worthy of respect and admiration as the women making a career, because both jobs require skill and concentration, and motherhood is for 24 hours a day, seven days a week.

Things happened very naturally with me and I became a career woman without knowing it. I just happened to have a baby and happened to have to bring her up, and I happened to have never married and got into a family situation. I happen to believe that she deserved the best, so I tried to get better jobs. I happened to get this job at Sunrise Home as a nurse aide and I went on from there with the experience of previous work to become a career woman, or a woman with a career, without even intending to.

Mind you, it wasn't so unusual because during the war many women had to go out to work, and although some of them went back home minding the children and family when their husbands came home, a lot didn't because they'd become very independent and they weren't going to go back and sit at home and twiddle their thumbs for anybody, not even their husbands. I think the women's movement would extend from those war years when women began to do responsible jobs in the army and in nursing. It was a whole different scene and I had drifted into it without being aware of women's rights or anything. I had no sympathy or very little sympathy with the aggressive feminists, but could understand very clearly what they were on about.

I can remember being so indignant when I was growing up about double standards to do with sex. It was accepted that men would feel the urge, and so if mother was in hospital, maybe having a baby, you blinked your eyes if he took off with the housemaid or something. You were very unwise if you left your sister or your housekeeper in with your husband. I look back on that now and I think women have just the same urges as men, but they weren't allowed to have an excuse. If he went off to the navy she wasn't allowed to have a little fling. I felt strongly about moral issues where there was unfairness.

I would say that it was easier for Lowana in that she didn't have to hide things. She didn't have to worry about somebody coming down the street who knew her. I never met anybody until I was well beyond caring what anybody thought, and then I started meeting quite a lot of my old friends and it didn't matter any more. I had no choice when I had her. There was no Domestic Purposes Benefit. There was family benefit which was a help, but the only kind of jobs you could do were domestic jobs in an institution or live-in jobs, and I was very fortunate. She went from house to house and that most likely gave her a better social sense – she always seemed more poised than I was. I was a very shy person, had a real inferiority complex. It wasn't until I kept Lowana and had to start managing that I improved. I wouldn't have been able to do the things at 17 that she did. She had got used to meeting people, living with them, getting to know them, and in a sense she had little bit of family life, in that there was always a family situation – well a sort of family situation.

We've always tried to be honest and I've always said to Lowana, 'If I've become possessive or interfering, you tell me.' I suppose there's only been about two or three times that I've said something and she's put me in my place. Another time she'll come to me for advice.

We've never ever had bad feelings about anything. We've always been able to work things through and in fact Lowana's been very good with me, quite wise at times. I used to – and still do occasionally – take on other people's problems and if she sees me doing it she will put me into order. She's quite a wise young lady and it's been a good relationship right through. I'd ask Lowana's advice on anything if I was stuck. I believe there's been times when she's been angry with me and there was only once where we parted company for a while but that wasn't a result of any row, it was just that we were thinking so differently.

All in all it has been very good relationship and I'm just grateful that Lowana's the kind of person that she is. I think she's done amazingly well and I'm very proud of her. She's always been very loyal, I can always come to her. I know that, and I can count on her husband too.

Lowana

I was born in St Mary's Hospital in Auckland in 1949. It's a place where young women who got themselves into trouble – a phrase my mother used for years – went to have their babies in secret. I had a really happy childhood. As I grew older and people talked about traumatic childhoods, I thought, well, mine was okay. People might feel sorry for me or whatever, but I never felt sorry for myself.

She took me to Tonga when I was two, I think, and I came back when I was six or seven with an aunty on a ship. I was just dying to see Mum. I can still remember the ship coming into the harbour and I didn't know who she was. She had to be pointed out to me. Later on, when I was about 10, I went to boarding school. I think those things had an effect on me but I didn't realise it at the time. As I was growing up I used to place quite a big distance between me and Mum and it wasn't really until I had kids that I closed that gap. Now I know more about rejection I realise that it was probably all tied up with that.

She hoped I would do well at school but I don't think she ever put any pressure on me at all. It was only in later years she said she had hoped for more because I was really a bit of a layabout.

I got pregnant the year after I left school so that probably fouled me up as far as anything for the future went. I was still living at home. We shared a bedroom and I remember creeping in at night and things like that. I remember Mum saying, 'Your period's overdue, gosh you're looking bloated this month', and I thought she'd sprung me, so I just said, 'I'm having a baby.' She was terribly upset when I told her but took it well. In fact, I remember not wanting to tell her because I knew she'd take it well. One of the things I resented about my darling mother when I was a teenager was that she was too good to be true and I didn't want to disappoint her. And around that time I had a huge feeling of responsibility towards her because I was her family. She didn't have a husband or other kids so I was very much the focus of her life. I probably exaggerated it in my own mind because she did have other interests and she loved her work, but it might be one reason why I broke out and got pregnant. She did take it well but she must have been quite heartbroken – she had taught me to be sensible and I wasn't.

I ended up going to Bethany in Auckland, but first I went and lived with some people doing their housework and that was horrible, a nightmare.

They were great at Bethany in their whole attitude towards adoption. They tried to handpick parents for your baby. There was a lot of secrecy in those days but they told us as much as they could without actually giving names so I had a fair idea where she went. She wasn't taken straight away, which was awful, and at that time I was blissfully ignorant of the after-effects of adopting her out. The baby had Tongan in her, so she was harder to adopt – blue-eyed blonde girls were the easiest. They said I could foster her until she got a home but I knew she could end up going from place to place and I didn't want that, so I just stayed in Bethany till she went to her home. It was about four weeks but felt more like six.

They let us take photos of the baby and look after it and we were able to name our children, even if the adoptive parents didn't keep the name, so at least I knew her and had something to grieve for. The staff kept in touch with the parents and we could write to Bethany and say, 'Have you heard how my baby is?' I did that for a couple of years which gave me the milestones. Then I gradually stopped writing. I just remembered her on birthdays and times like that. But my reaction was really terrible. Because I didn't know about grief and loss I just used to go out and get really drunk and I was a bit promiscuous for a few years.

I wished in later years that Mum had encouraged me to keep the baby, but on the other hand I'm glad she didn't. There's lots of reasons for that. There still wasn't a benefit and I knew that I wasn't the sort to be able to cope with going round housekeeping. Just the short stint I did while I was pregnant was enough. I was probably more bolshie than her – more likely to get fired. And of course you truly believe that your child is going to a home where they'll give her everything that you can't provide – though even I knew that love and affection is what she needed most. I've been fortunate because I met my daughter two or three years ago and we keep in touch. She's had a good life – a life that suited somebody who belongs to me.

Then six years later I got pregnant again. This time I kept the baby. There was no doubt about it. I think I got pregnant almost deliberately.

I had had all sort of jobs in between the two pregnancies. I worked in a medical lab for ages, then I went psychopedic nursing. I had grown up in the Sunrise Home for Blind Children and had always been fascinated by the mentally retarded kids so I went psychopedic nursing and really enjoyed it. But the ratio of staff to patients is crazy and I didn't like the system at all. I wasn't mature enough to think, 'Well, I'll just put up with the system', so I left. It's a shame I didn't have the tenacity to finish things. It's probably partly a character trait but it's a pain when you're 40 before you decide what you want to do.

I kept in touch with Mum over those six years, although there were times when I didn't see much of her and felt that my friends were my family. I was in my twenties and flatting, getting into dope, nightclubbing and just having a good time really. I couldn't stick at a job long enough to save the money to go overseas like other people – that's something I do regret. I said I didn't need to, that everybody would come to me, which was a pretty stupid thing to say!

At one stage I went off hitch-hiking round the South Island on my own. I was always very independent and that might have been something to do with the way Mum brought me up. Because we moved around a lot I didn't have an established base or a room of my own. I was quick to get out of home not because I hated Mum, but because I wanted my own space. My poor mother, you know she never nagged me about hitch-hiking. She just used to say, 'Well, be careful and ring me.' It was a wonderful, special holiday – finding myself, writing bits of poetry. It's something I've done, it's all in there but I've got no desire to do it all again. A lot of people are doing it now for the first time in their forties and I think, 'Oh dear, I'm glad it's not me. I'm glad I built up my personal philosophy back then.'

When I became pregnant again, I can remember ringing Mum and telling her I was having a baby because I wanted to let her know really firmly that I knew what I was doing. I was sorry I wasn't married but I felt I could bring up a child. I went on about 'fatherless being better than fighting parents, surely'. She seemed to be okay about it, but I didn't want to know if she wasn't. I was doing something for me – I was probably quite selfish about it really. Anyway, the father of that child is the man I'm married to now. It's wonderful. It was never intended. I'd always really, really loved him but when I got pregnant he was already on his way to do his OE.

I moved in with various friends who took care of me. Mum was really supportive although I didn't include her a lot. She has the knack of being able to keep her distance if that's what's needed. Now that I'm a mother, I think she was amazing. I'd be far more interfering. She never came on with the 'my grandchild' bit, but she was quite excited.

Mum had a great change when she was in her 40s. She decided to go and live on faith and ran a crash-pad in Ponsonby with some other people. They had no income and she'd given away all her material possessions – I got her TV. I was really proud of her but her work colleagues used to get right up my nose. I'd go round and they'd say, 'How are you?' I'd say, 'Fine', and they'd say, 'Praise the Lord.' I couldn't have a conversation with anybody except her there and I didn't really approve of the people she was with. But by the time my son was born she had moved to another place and I felt more at home there. As soon as I had the baby I started seeing more of her. It wasn't that I used her to babysit, it was just that connection between us. I used to walk down with the pram and leave the baby with her for a couple of hours and go shopping or whatever. I remember at one stage I tried working and she babysat but that didn't work very well because he really was too young.

I found it quite hard on my own. He was quite an easy baby but as he got older he was a bit more difficult. I moved into the bottom half of her place and just loved it. They were all going 'Alleluia' upstairs and I was doing my own thing downstairs. Of course it was neat for my son because he was able to move up and down.

It was while I was there that I became a Christian. I had resisted the whole thing, partly because I was looking for my own spiritual path and partly because she was a Christian and I had a horror of being like my mother. I loved her and respected her, but I didn't want to be like her, even though I could see the patterns being repeated. I was trying to shy away from it, which was silly because I could never be like her – we're completely different in our outlook and our nature. So when I became a Christian it must have been really neat for her and I didn't care by then because it was my choice.

I went to her church and liked it although sometimes I used to think they got a bit carried away. I stopped going after a while. I found it very difficult because I am a free thinker. I know that as a Christian the stuff in the Bible is considered absolute, but there are still things I question and I find that every church I go to there's just so much dogma. Yet I don't want to throw away my faith which has stood me in good stead, especially when my kids were little. It was the thread that kept me together many times. I enjoy being with people who believe the same things, but I never seem able to find a church that I'm comfortable in. But that doesn't bother me any more.

The Quaker boarding school I went to probably gave me more than anybody's ever given me besides Mum in the way of a desire for spiritual truth – not that I was really aware of it at the time. We were always having silence: before you started your meal you always had a minute's silence; at the beginning of assembly you had 10 minutes' silence; when you went to bed it was silence, and you were put on silence if you talked to much. The discipline that came from that must have been really important. I like to have that peace.

I didn't have boyfriends after I had the baby. I didn't want my kid to be having a series of men flipping in and out. It was Mum's strong moral influence again. She had given me stability by not doing that herself. Even when she went to a concert with somebody I used to get really frightened that she'd fall in love and get married and leave me behind, so I wonder what it must be like for those kids whose parents do let men take over their lives.

I was on the DPB and survived quite well. I didn't do a lot, just looked after the baby. I went to a playcentre for a while but didn't fit in that well. There were lots of feminists, quite political people, and I wasn't at all political. I've realised since I've moved down here and got into community work that when you're living in a place like inner-city Auckland there are radical people who do it for you. Anyway, I didn't feel passionately about what was going on in our country. It would have disturbed my happy little life. I was into baking bread and trying to grow vegetables, struggling with the clay. But I soon realised that I wasn't going to be the earth mother ideal which was prevalent at the time and which I really thought I wanted. I'd been brought up with children so I thought I'd be a really neat mother, but it was in an institutional environment, it wasn't at all natural. I never adapted to the housewife role properly, though I felt better about that when I realised that I never actually had a model to work on.

My son grew up and went to kindy and then school. About that time his father came back from overseas. He was just going to come here for a couple of months to see his parents and the baby, and I was just there, I suppose. But it was really funny – it was a whole Mills and Boon situation. We fell in love, not having done that the first time round, and he's still here, four more boys later!

We got married at home and struggled away in Auckland. My husband bought a restaurant and I kept getting pregnant! We came down here to Hawke's Bay when I was pregnant with the fourth one. We were sick of city life and I'd always wanted to escape to a better climate. But I hated it. Mum decided to come and live with us for six months because it was going to be a lot of work getting it together. My husband was never home, he was working phenomenal hours, and I had encountered racism for the first time in my life. It was really hideous so it was good having her there as a sort of stable grandma. We were almost too dependent on her sometimes and she always worried about that, yet in those first years I think we'd have fallen apart if she hadn't been here. I know about co-dependence and I think there is a certain amount of co-dependency there, but I also believe we're here to help each other and that families are for support.

After we'd been here a while Mum decided that she'd like to stay in Hawke's Bay. She liked the change of pace from Auckland, she had a sister here and she was making friends, so she got herself a place to live and we continued to live on our own.

Although I hated the place for years, we couldn't get out

because we were so broke. Those first three or four years here were probably the worst in my life and I'm just glad that Mum was there. I had my little bit of faith to hang on to and I had her to help me with the kids when I just couldn't handle it – I had no one else to turn to. In fact, a couple of times over those years when I just cracked she and my husband came to the party really quickly, shipped me out of town and got people to look after the kids. I don't know what I would have done without her. I suppose we would have coped, but we could quite easily have blown apart, so I'm really thankful for her faith in my husband being able to make it eventually, and in her love for me. It really held us together.

It's good that that saga is over now, that there isn't that huge need for each other's support and we're just mates again. She's got her own exciting independent life and I've got mine.

I began coming out of my misery when we moved from the country into town. I started emerging from the nappies and getting into things, and again it was really neat because both Mum and my husband supported me into getting back into work and starting again. I had a woman to help me with the housework and we were talking about being tied to the house and stress and so on and she told me about a place in Palmerston North called Parentline. She said, 'It's a shame there isn't one here.' Because I was still so raw from my experience of being lonely and stressed as a parent, I said, 'Why don't you start one? I'm sure it must be easy to do it. I'll support you and give you a hand.' So she and I rang the other Parentline and made millions of phone calls and got one started. I don't know how we did it. Caring for the kids would all fall back on Mum and my husband, but they let me do it and gave me the space.

From that I joined several committees and went through a committee phase which lasted about a year. While I was on the COGS (Community Organisations Grants Scheme) committee, the COGS co-ordinator was looking for a clerical worker, so I got that job and learned a lot there. I'd lost a lot of confidence in my ability to get up and say what I thought. The woman I worked with was really strong and stroppy and wonderful and she gave me back a lot of my confidence. Now I'm the co-ordinator for Parentline on the administrative side, 20 hours a week, and love the job.

There's lots of similarities between Mum's life and mine – getting pregnant is the obvious one, I suppose. But other things too – she discovered what she wanted to do in her forties and I've done the same, although I still see myself changing quite a bit before I'm 60 and that's okay. The direction is still a people direction which is similar to her, and that probably goes back generations. Mum always taught me to care for others and it's always been important to me.

There are differences between our lives too. I've married and had heaps of kids and I'm more socially outgoing. I'll go to a pub and hear a band occasionally, for example. Because of her upbringing and her beliefs she probably met people in different places to me. I'm more worldly and I'm much louder in voicing my opinions about things than she is. She was always a bit scared to do that, whereas I've never known much fear about anything. Well, since I've had kids I've been scared of aeroplanes and stuff like that, but that's survival – maternal instinct stuff. Mum's more humble than me and in some ways that's more positive, but it can be negative. She puts herself down more than she needs to. I've inherited a bit of that trait but I've tried to stop it. She puts the needs of others too much ahead of her own needs, whereas I've learnt that that's back to front sometimes. She was never intolerant of other people's views and I think that's one of the best things she's given me – people are just people and that's it. It's not my place to change them.

People used to say to me, 'You're so close to your Mum', but I'm not always that close. There's tons of things I haven't told her and there's still a few things I'm almost too scared to tell her – that's the little girl in me. But it's really only in a couple of areas, and I know other people who have that in lots of areas, so I suppose it is a good relationship. I think your relationship with your mother really improves anyway later on in life and she gets on really well with my husband, too, which helps. I know lots of women who have good relationships with their mothers. It's an important connection.

Alice & Kate

I talked to Alice and Kate together, an experience that was never less than entertaining as they discussed their lives together and reflected on the changes they have made.

Kate's life has included an experience of anorexia, which she now attributes partly to her need to separate from the family and establish her own identity and partly to a slow realisation that a traditional marriage was not for her. She has been much happier as a lesbian. In contrast, Alice has evolved her identity within her marriage. She has worked all her life, at first from her own hairdressing salon and later from home. This has meant she has always had some money of her own and been able to make some independent choices.

Alice's remarkable openness to new ideas has enabled her to accept her daughter's choices without judgement or pain. She obviously enjoys her daughter's company and appreciates the intimacy women can share, saying to Kate, 'You've been so much happier and more yourself, which you can be with another woman. You don't seem to be able to do that with a man, you have to pussyfoot around them.'

Alice and Kate

ALICE: I was born at a little place called Silverhope in the Manawatu. Mum married Dad when she was 21. He had been married before and his wife had died, so he was 17 years older than Mum and already had five children, ranging from a baby to about 12 years old. I don't remember them very much, except for one boy who always championed me when my brothers teased me. He died when he was 21 of cerebral meningitis. There were eight of us in the second family – 13 children altogether – so Mum was pretty busy. And I'm sure it must have been hard for her to come into a very closed country neighbourhood with lots of inter-relationships and a lot of fighting and feuding. She felt bound to keep the house shining like a new pin and still be a perfect wife and mother. She was very artistic and a divine pastry-maker and won lots of competitions.

When I was in my early teens we moved to Palmerston North because Dad had lost the farms in the slump. Mum left him some time after we moved there, but later she took him back and nursed him till he died of cancer. She'd had a late baby who was only three and a half when Dad died. The widow's pension was pitiful so Mum opened a home cookery and tearooms where I helped her. She worked day and night at that shop and one day my little brother got out of the yard, wandered away and was hit by a car. He was so badly injured the doctors thought he would die. He lived, but he was in a coma for a long time. Mum never left the hospital, and she never went back to the shop. She lived to be 98 but never achieved anything much for herself, even though she had so much potential.

I came in the middle of the second family. I got on all right with Mum in the early days – I just took things for granted. She was busy and did for me what was needed. She loved us of course, but she was fairly straight-laced – I suppose it was the era. I don't think I was ever what she wanted. I think I was a bit of a tomboy and she wanted a lady-like daughter, more like my sister. Being in the middle of a large family is a very lonely place to be – you do miss your mother's attention and a little cuddle and a kiss, and Mum never did that. She always said that she loved babies but she couldn't cuddle us as we grew older. She wasn't a warm person.

I remember when I was about 12 and we were living in Palmerston North, the neighbours' nephew used to come and visit them in the holidays. He was about the same age as me or a bit older so we had a 'thing' going. One day he gave me a little kiss – that's all it was. Some time later I must have been a bit off-colour or emotional. In those days I think that mothers thought you were doing things you shouldn't in the hayloft! Of course I hadn't been, but she'd never told me anything about sex. All she'd said was, 'Never let a man be familiar with you', and I didn't know what she meant. When I kissed this boy, she quizzed me about whether I'd been up to something. I knew she meant having a baby and I said, 'No', but then I must have gone to bed – I was a plump little girl – and felt my stomach, thinking, 'It's getting a bit fat.' When Mum came into the bedroom, I don't remember what I said to her, but it was something about my stomach. She just said, 'Oh', and went out of the room and nothing more was said. To this day I don't know whether she thought we'd done something. I wish I could have told her in later life that I hadn't been a naughty girl. She couldn't have handled talking about it and if she couldn't handle something she wouldn't mention it again.

I don't know that we ever understood or got very close to each other, not woman to woman. I didn't see an awful lot of her once I left home. After I married she would come for visits, of course, but they were really short. She was marvellous at dropping everything and coming to one or the other of us when we needed her, like when we had babies. I think she still loved us in her own way and there was nothing she wouldn't do for us.

KATE: Gran wasn't warm and giving but she did the best she could. She didn't have a happy life. She was very much a survivor and a fighter, I think. She did really well to do what she did, given her circumstances. You have a warmth and you're much more demonstrative than Gran ever was, but you've got that other part as well – the survival and fighting part.

ALICE: I went first to Silverhope School which had about 30 pupils, then Ashhurst School. At such a little school no one took much interest in what we were doing, but I got through school fairly well – I was even dux! I don't know that Mum had any great expectations of me, so I left when I was 12 after I got Proficiency. It was in the middle of the 1930s Depression, Dad had died, and Mum couldn't afford to buy school uniforms so I left. The only job I could get was doing domestic work. I did that for a while till Woolworths opened in Palmerston North and I worked there for quite a few years. Then because I'd always been interested in hairdressing Mum suggested that I take some night classes, and after that I went into hairdressing.

About that time I moved to Wellington for a while with my sister. I was 18 and I wanted to leave home – everybody else seemed to be doing it. I think Mum was reasonably happy about it, it was probably one less to worry about. We had a room on the Terrace. In those days you had a room and cooking conveniences that you shared with other people in the house – nowhere to entertain or anything. But it was great, I enjoyed life.

I met my husband when I was 21. It was New Years' Eve 1940, and I was back in Palmerston North. In those days we used to go to the Post Office to see the New Year in, and I met him there. We got married two years later. I don't think Mum ever thought there was any man good enough for her daughters but she was fine about it. I expected to get married. I think I was always on the look-out for somebody nice!

We lived in New Plymouth for a while after James came back from the war, then bought a hairdressing business. He had been a baker before the war, which he hated, so we ran the salon together and he learned some of the rudiments of hairdressing, enough to help out. He could do perms and take bookings – because that's quite an art in itself – and sweep the floor and do the laundry. I had two children while we had the salon, so it meant that I could be home and just go down to the salon when I was needed. James could run the business as long as he had staff who could do all the hairdressing. When I had to go down he would stay home and be 'housemother', so I would say he was one of the first house-husbands. It was very successful.

KATE: I remember that story you tell about him being introduced as Mr Alice Stewart – I don't know how he reacted to that.

ALICE: I don't think he liked it much and I didn't like it either because I felt that it diminished him. I liked the business life and having a salon meant that I could intertwine work and children if I had to. But if he hadn't been able to look after the children it wouldn't have been so easy. After a while I found it tiring and he was ready to get into some sort of work of his own where he'd be Mr James Stewart. He looked around for a business and I stayed home and looked after the children. I enjoyed it, I was ready to stop.

We had four children – a son, then three daughters. I was pleased to have girls, I really was. In some ways I would have liked to have had another son, but it didn't work out that way and nobody seemed to regret it at all.

The girls and I had our moments, but our relationship was fairly good, I thought. I was never quite sure how much I should find out or where the middle line was. You want to get through and get to know your daughters better, but that doesn't seem to come until they're grown up and you're all women together. Well, that's how it was in our house.

I worked off and on all the time I had children – I did a bit of hairdressing at home. I still do even now.

KATE: You worked steadily – you were fully booked and I can remember you working for IHC and doing meals-on-wheels. I remember you doing community work as well as hairdressing.

ALICE: All my married life I had my own money. I got a housekeeping allowance from James, but basically I worked for the extras like music lessons and going to university. But, even though I had that money, I've never been independent in the sense that I would buy things without consulting him. I haven't got that much push. In those days you didn't do anything without consulting your husband because it diminished him. Now I can see that that's all wrong.

KATE: It was easy being Mum's daughter. I think because I was the oldest girl we were always quite close. I very much got on with my life in terms of playing with my friends, playing sport and all those kind of things. Mum was always there supporting me, making sure I was where I needed to be, that I had the gear and that meals were cooked or she'd keep meals for me. I was the helpful one, being the eldest. We spent of lot of time in the kitchen preparing meals together, doing dishes and Saturday morning cleaning – it gave us a lot of time and opportunity to talk. I don't remember us having any great storms or anxieties or anything like that. She had that more with my sisters. They were more temperamental.

ALICE: I think that you held a lot back, though. You weren't very demanding, you didn't ask.

KATE: I could see the stresses that were there with the others – the years when Judith was sick and things like that – but I didn't feel deprived, it was just the way things were. My life felt quite full and I felt loved and cared for.

We enjoyed each other's company and I always talked about what was going on for me. I still do that now. I remember Mum saying two things to me in my teenage years. Once I was standing in the laundry and Mum was doing the washing – I must have been about 14, I suppose – and she said, 'I don't think marriage should be for ever.' I thought, 'This is interesting.' The other was something about, 'Did I ever feel that I missed out by being a girl? Did I wish I was a boy?', or 'Did I think that boys had it easier?' I'd never thought about it at that stage. I was a tomboy and I just did everything the boys did. I wasn't aware then of the inequities. I was very competitive with them and could meet them on their own terms.

ALICE: I don't think that meant that I wished I was a man. I certainly don't remember saying it.

KATE: I imagine you were bending over the washing machine, washing for three hours on a Saturday morning, having put in a hard week.

ALICE: It might have been one of my 'crying into the

washing water days' when you're so depressed and busy and things aren't going so well and you're thinking there must be more to life than this!

KATE: I don't remember having any particular goals as a child but when I was in the sixth form I got really fed up with school. I came home in the first term and said I wanted to leave. Dad went off and looked for work for me. He came home one night and said, 'I've got you a job in the bank.' My sheer horror at the thought of working in a bank and settling down in Napier was more than I could cope with, so I went back to school. At the end of the year I went and saw the guidance counsellor who said, 'You're good at sport, why don't you go to Phys Ed School?', so I did. I didn't ask any questions and I really had no concept of what university was like. It was very near to the closing time for applications so everything got filled in in a great hurry. I was 17.

I think Dad would have been quite happy if all of us had left school early – I think the ultimate for him was to leave school and work in a bank. He didn't have the same awareness or expectations for us as Mum. My perception was that Mum was much more supportive of us doing those things like going to university.

ALICE: It was because he had left school early, as I did, and had gone to work. I don't think he realised that times were so different and you didn't have to do that now. I don't know why I was different. My mother would have had ambitions for us that filtered through and I talked to all my women friends. As the girls were growing up they had friends who were going to university, everybody was going.

KATE: It was the door to the future.

ALICE: I felt awful when Kate went off to university. She was so far away. We went down together to Dunedin and she lived in a grotty old place. She organised it by letter and she had no idea of what she was going into. I hated that. We used to write about every three days for a while.

KATE: For a long time I think we wrote every day.

ALICE: I remember the first year that you were there. It was Easter and I sent you the money to fly home, not thinking that you probably didn't get that much time off from university. You shouldn't have come at all, but you were pretty homesick. It was probably a good thing in the long run because you felt better when you went back, but James thought I was dreadful, sending you all this money to fly home. I couldn't have done it without having my own money.

KATE: I remember us going into the post office and you taking out the family benefit to give me – £200 to go to university!

ALICE: Dad thought the family benefit paid for everything!

KATE: I did phys ed and met Richard six months after I arrived – on his twentieth birthday. I was really desperate, really lonely and shy. Everyone seemed so confident and capable. We got engaged, then disengaged 18 months later, and eventually married.

I went flatting after two terms and in my second year became anorexic, although it wasn't recognised then as anorexia. I just got thinner and thinner and went down to a dangerously low weight.

ALICE: I talked to the doctor about it and he pooh-poohed the idea. I knew she wasn't well. I hadn't given it a name but she got to the stage where she simply couldn't eat.

KATE: I think it was the whole image of women at that time – it was the Twiggy era.

ALICE: It was something to do with the shock of going away and being totally on your own.

KATE: It could have been, but it was more about being the right shape. I'd been big at school – I was ten and a half stone even though I was very active. I was eight and a half when I went to university and I went down to six and a half. Some days I could hardly drag myself to lectures.

ALICE: Then you did your teachers' training and when you were doing a teaching section one of the teachers rang and asked me if you were quite well. I didn't want to land you in any trouble, so I think I carried it a bit. You weren't well and you were so thin. You hadn't really come right at all.

KATE: I don't think I recognised what it was then. I was really aware of the effect it was having on my friendships and my mental and physical health. Looking back I must have looked terrible but that's one of the things about anorexia – you think you look fine. It took me a long time to eat properly and it's probably only in the last eight or 10 years that I've come right.

ALICE: Your periods stopped, didn't they? And we thought you weren't going to be able to have any children.

KATE: That part didn't bother me. I was very focused on academic achievement. I got straight As and I think part of that was because I felt there was an expectation that I wouldn't do well. Because I'd gone from the sixth form and I'd never been a particularly high achiever academically at school, people were just waiting for me to fail and I was going to show them! I am very tenacious. There's nothing that gets me going more than people thinking I can't do something.

I went down to Dunedin to graduation, then married Richard.

ALICE: Neither James nor I wanted you to marry but I don't think we ever made any objection. I think you would have married him anyway – you just said you were tenacious! I didn't think that you and Richard knew each other. But this was the thing that women did – they married.

KATE: I was 21 and I can remember quite consciously thinking, 'No one else might want to marry me.' It wasn't that I loved him but that no one else might want me and I might be left on the shelf. Such were the social messages we were fed. Isn't it terrible? I thought I'd better take the opportunity and having made that decision I thought, 'I've got to make it work.' I remember saying to Mum at the time, 'Don't worry about us, we'll be fine.'

We lived in Christchurch initially and I had Ben there against all odds. When he was a year old we moved to Blenheim and I taught, because I found being at home really hard, not fulfilling and not my scene at all. Richard stayed home with Ben. He didn't want to work any more anyway, so it suited him. I did that for two years, then I desperately wanted to have another child. When I conceived, Richard had to get another job and that wasn't very easy because in those days men just didn't step in and out of the workforce. Eventually he did get one and we moved to Marton where I had Nick and Kim. I stayed at home most of that time and immersed myself in the kids. I loved it – read to them and played with them. Mum and I kept in touch. We wrote and she'd come and stay from time to time.

ALICE: But I found I had to change my type of letter after you married. Letters for us would just be a conversation piece, just little thoughts that we'd had about something – you understand things between yourselves. But if you're conscious that the man's going to read it and think, 'Oh what drivel all this is, the woman's mad', then you get more stilted and formal.

Our relationship didn't change all that much when the children were born. I always felt happy if I was wanted to help out. I went to all the children when they had their babies.

KATE: I was quite possessive. I think I made it hard for you to do as much as you wanted. I wasn't good at letting people help me and I kept you at arm's length because I thought that was a reflection on my ability to cope. Our relationship was fine at that time, though a bit distanced, but I certainly didn't make it easy in that respect.

ALICE: That's true, even with things like doing housework or getting meals I think you always felt that you should be doing it yourself. I was there to help you and I suppose I felt a bit resentful at times and wondered what I was doing there, but it passed. It's all forgotten now.

KATE: Then one day, when Kim was about one – I was 28, I had Ben at school and two pre-schoolers – I remember standing at the kitchen sink, thinking, 'God, my life's ended. I'm going to be 33 before I get back to work.' I was a playcentre mum, I was on the kindergarten committee and I went to Parents' Centre, but I wanted to do something more. Part of that was an awareness of feminism as well as something for my own needs. I did a Diploma in Education through Massey and a two-year Certificate in Counselling. I studied around the kids – getting up at five in the morning – so I was free during the day for them.

About that time I began to realise the marriage wasn't working. I tried to talk to Richard, but he didn't want to know. At first I wasn't particularly interested in leaving. I think I denied the difficulties for a long time – it was the old thing of 'You make your bed, you lie on it.' I'd married this man for whatever reason and I had to make it work. I had to prove that I could do it right. But eventually I said, 'The only thing we have in common is the children.'

ALICE: There was a certain shame if your marriage ended. It was always thought in the past that it was a woman's fault if the marriage ended.

KATE: It was more out of sheer tenacity. And in a way it was easier to stay than to go – I didn't know about the DPB and things like that. Over that time I immersed myself in work – I had three part-time jobs. Richard didn't actively resist my doing it but he didn't do anything to make it easier either in terms of helping. So I was still doing the cooking and the shopping and the kids. I didn't ever have a weekend where he'd take the kids and I could just be there. It was a form of passive resistance. That's where I got to the point where I said, 'I've had enough. If I want to get on with my life I've got to leave.'

We both ended up going to Palmerston North and it was while I was studying there that I met a woman who said, 'We need a co-ordinator for Women's Refuge and you're just the person.' I didn't know anything about domestic violence at that stage, but I said, 'Great.' Another dive in the deep end. I remember the first case I went to was a young Maori woman who had been very severely beaten – she had gouges all down her back, her face was all bruised, her teeth were knocked out and her eyeballs had been gouged. She was just a mess and she had a baby girl.

So Refuge took over my life. I worked on call, so it was often 18 hours a day. Richard ran the household and I came and went. Looking back, I probably didn't see a hell of a lot of the kids. I became absolutely focused on what I discovered happens to women – the abuse and the violence and the awful situations that women live in. That was a really intense year and at the end I crawled out exhausted. My next job was as a community worker. I also did some social work papers at Massey. I was driven really. I'd found something that hit me at the core, probably for the first time.

ALICE: I saw a great change in you. I thought at the time you'd become harder and you weren't such a nice person to know. I didn't really like the change, although I now recognise it as toughness, or strength. Older people were slightly suspicious of assertive women then, because assertiveness was just appearing. And you were so busy. The last time we came to see you, you were always dashing out to some crisis or answering the phone. I wondered whether that had an effect on your marriage, but I realise now that the marriage was not good anyway.

KATE: I think Refuge often gets blamed for that. People label refuge workers, saying, 'They're all lesbians anyway.' It's a form of controlling all women by labelling them.

Coming to terms with my own sexuality was quite a long process which began while I was married. I became aware that I didn't want relationships with men any more. At that time I didn't know how to meet other lesbians, because most of them were being 'normal' like me; the people I knew were lesbians didn't appeal to me. That's when I thought, 'I'll be a political lesbian. I won't have relationships with men but because I don't know what the next step is, I'm not going to have relationships with women either.'

My outing came at a Refuge conference where the issue of lesbians hiding behind heterosexual privilege was a big thing. At that point I didn't know whether I was or wasn't lesbian. It just came gradually and I did what felt right for that me at the time. I wasn't particularly out and open, except to my close friends.

I moved to Wellington to work. My first lover came down soon after that and we started to live together. That became my way of life.

I didn't make the grand announcement to Mum and Dad, although I told my sisters. My sister in Australia was absolutely horrified and said I should rethink it and what was I doing to Mum and Dad, what a terrible thing this was and how could I? I had made it clear that if she had difficulties with it that was her problem, she had to work it through. It was two years before she said she'd given it some thought and it was okay.

ALICE: When Kate's marriage ended we were there to support her if she needed it, with money or whatever. The worst part was when you went to Wellington – that was a bad time because we couldn't support you in any way.

KATE: I had a lot going on for me then, being lesbian and leaving the children with Richard. I'd had them for two years on my own and he decided that he could parent them better than I could and wanted to do his liberal father bit.

I didn't communicate much with you for about six months except very briefly and I remember getting desperate letters saying, 'At least let me know that you're okay.' It was like I just cut myself off.

ALICE: It worried me that I didn't have an address. I still don't know where you lived – maybe in the park. That was awful because I had absolutely no communication with you at all. I didn't know what was happening. I wasn't happy about Richard having the children, because I still don't like the idea of the father having the children somehow – it seems the wrong way round. Perhaps that's old-fashioned, but it's the way I feel. We were very angry with Richard, his lack of caring and support for you. Moneywise he always seemed to be a bit tight, but that's a common story, isn't it? But we were there for support as needed.

Our son had already had a divorce so I was sorry when Kate's marriage ended. At that time it seemed that all around people were finishing their marriages, whether they were 20 or 50 or even 70. Both of us supported Kate. Dad's been great. It's not that you get used to it, but it's there and it's a reality. And strangely enough as we've got older we've found we like to be involved and to help where we can, but when we're just on our own together we don't dwell on things or let them trouble us. We let it flow over us and hope that if the kids want anything they'll let us know – and I think they do.

KATE: You said that you never quite knew how much to ask, but you always had an ability to be open to what you heard. You kept the lines of communication open without asking prying questions so it always felt really safe. You were always very non-judgemental with what you heard. Sometimes I imagine you heard things that threw you a bit, but you were always there, able to support and not judge, to not show disappointment or any of those things. It was really great.

ALICE: What we would have once called taking sides. I don't know whether it's a skill because it's not conscious, it's nothing special.

KATE: It's certainly something that's been a good model for me with my kids, not that I've managed to do it as well as I'd like to, but I always remember how much it meant to me.

ALICE: And I have to say Kate supported me and my husband when we were having a very bad time. He was really difficult to live with for a while and I came down here several times, which is a bit of a turnaround. And yet I don't think I made you feel any less love for Dad, because I didn't want to. I didn't mean that you had to take sides or anything.

It was a strange time. He was having a sort of male menopause. He always used to go quiet – what we used to call sulking – but there was one period where he barely spoke to me for six months. I never did know what it was. We had a bach at that time and it got so bad I said, 'If I'm so awful to live with, why don't you go there? Don't expect me to go because I'm not going to.' I thought, 'If he doesn't like what's happening, he can go.' It was his birthday a while later, so I weakened and went up and he looked dreadful. I was glad I went, it did change things and now we have a very good relationship. I don't think he could put his finger on what it was – although he'd just retired so maybe that had something to do with it.

And he was the only male in this all-female household, because Greg had been gone for years. I suppose he felt a bit neglected at times, but he never ever expressed anything. He always said, 'You can express things and I can't.'

KATE: When you came to stay we talked about setting you up in a hairdressing business. It wasn't what you wanted but it was good to explore options, to say, 'These are the possibilities, what choice do you want to make?'

KATE: Mum found out that I was lesbian by chance when my lover and I stayed at the lake.

ALICE: It was just the tone of voice, an endearment or something. I don't think I had any idea before that, I'm sure I hadn't thought of it, but when I knew it didn't worry me at all, not in the slightest. I'd never thought about lesbian relationships really, but it didn't trouble me and strangely enough it never troubled James either. I didn't say anything to him at the time, but much later on – four or five years later – it came out that he really had known that too.

KATE: We never really discussed it, but Mum and Dad came and stayed with us often. We'd just move out of our bedroom and go downstairs because it was easier. Initially we'd 'de-dyke' the house – we took all the photos away, etc – but after a couple of times we didn't even bother doing that, we were quite open. Then Mum and I talked about it. I gave Mum some articles to read and she talked to my youngest sister who had always been very positive about it so we were able to be quite open about our relationship.

ALICE: And when you stayed with us you shared a bed and Dad would bring you cups of tea. It was quite normal for us but I didn't discuss it with anyone else. I do have to say that it's not a subject I bring up with other people because I'm not really sure how women of my generation generally feel about it.

KATE: You did comment about a friend who'd lived with a woman for years. Her partner had got ill and died and suddenly there was a connection made for you – maybe that's what their relationship was – and you realised how hard it must have been for her with the lack of acknowledgement about what the relationship meant.

I think it's neat the way that Mum's able to incorporate my lesbianism into her life. Especially when I think of the number of lesbians who aren't able to tell their parents and who live a sort of semi-life of secrecy because they fear loss of parental love and support. I've been able to be fully myself for the last eight years because you've known and accepted it and fully accepted my lover, and that's great. She's part of the family.

ALICE: It's been a good change for you. You've been so much happier and more yourself, which you can be with another woman. You don't seem to be able to do that with a man, you have to pussyfoot around them.

KATE: When I was growing up I got a lot of support from Mum and the freedom to be who I was. I remember once when I was quite young, putting on a leopardskin velvety skirt that I'd made with black stockings and make-up and walking out into the kitchen, probably expecting, even hoping for a response, and Mum didn't even look up. I said, 'I'm just going into the library', and she didn't turn a hair, so I went back and changed! It looked awful! I just wanted a response and didn't get it. I think of that when my daughter looks her most bizarre.

Mum was a good model of an independent woman. She's been a model too in terms of the way that she raised and disciplined us. She was open so that we could talk. There's been heaps of learning for me in the way that she always worked and has to a large extent been her own person. And her tenacity. Although I do think having the close relationship we did was a contributing factor to my anorexia – the difficulty I had in breaking away and becoming separate, stepping outside of that and saying, 'This is who I am.' I think the move to Palmerston was the start of that – no longer being the one who just goes along and doesn't cause ripples. Somewhere along the line I must have decided I'd prove that Mum and Dad were good parents by being good, having a good marriage, achieving and so on, because my brother had been so difficult. That affected my expectations, it was part of my being driven – that and my passion.

ALICE: You always tried to be all things to all people. Now you're yourself and a much nicer person, not holding things back like you might have done once. In your teens you were almost too good to be true.

KATE: Real superwoman stuff! Over the last 10 years I've learnt to let go, especially in the last two years. I'm much more able to ask for help now. Although Mum's support and tolerance has always been there, I haven't often asked for it. We haven't had prolonged fights or bust-ups. We've been able to heal rifts.

ALICE: I think mothers keep the family together without ever seeming to. Once the mother's gone, for whatever reason, there's no one to keep the family together and make things right again.

It's very much more open in families now. In the past children haven't really known their parents because the parents presented this good side to their kids as an example of how their children should be. They didn't show themselves as caring human beings. The lines were so rigid that naturally children fought against them, because that's the way children are. Now children can get on well in their families. They don't have to be seen and not heard, they can have their say.

Having daughters is wonderful. I suppose being females together, you have a rapport or whatever you like to call it. I know there are some mothers who don't get on with their daughters terribly well, and I wonder why, but I think it must come from both sides. Their natures obviously conflict. With the three girls and me, I think it's something to do with not living too close together. As a parent you can get too involved in their lives, and perhaps if they've got husbands their husbands resent their coming to you. Men are possessive. So perhaps it's because we've never all lived in the same town that we can come together and be close. We don't make demands on the children, we don't expect them to come home for Christmas and things like that, although we think it's nice if they do.

When all the children had left home, we were quite happy to be on our own. After all, the children weren't far away and I was happy as long as I could keep in touch. We were pretty tired by this stage. We'd both worked all our lives. We weren't young parents – I was 29 when I had my first child and I had my last one when I was 38 – so it had been a very busy time. We didn't do anything very revolutionary, we just turned more to each other. But I love the grandkids. I don't know them very well. I'd dearly love to be close enough to have them come in and out and have a biscuit – do the things grandmothers do.

I'm more contented now and more myself than I've ever been in my life. Through life I've craved material things, like a nice house and possessions, which James didn't. Now it doesn't matter so much. I can look at things and think, 'That's nice', and not want them.

I think women need to press on and become themselves, not wanting to be equal to men but maybe separate. It will take a lot of time, because I don't think men want to change. They're not changing very fast. I guess it will take a generation or two to change.

Jeanette & Hilary

Jeanette and Hilary are just the right women to end this book. Both are perceptive observers of social change and each tells her own story with warmth and honesty. While they may have had more than their fair share of distressing experiences, they have survived them through courage, mutual support and tolerance.

Like Alice in the previous story, Jeanette has been open to new ideas and new ways. Her ability to see things in context has enabled her to maintain a close relationship with all five of her children as they have gone in different directions. Hilary appreciates her mother's support and acceptance, while acknowledging the differences between her own life and her mother's. It's a happy balance.

Jeanette

We were a middle-class family, a family of four daughters in a small country town — middle between town and country, middle of the social scale. It was probably never said, but I think we absorbed the expectation, as children do almost by osmosis, that our main purpose in life was to get married, and having children was definitely part of it. You could see the way men talked about single women – as if they were a kind of second-class citizen, as if they hadn't made it. A child absorbs so many unspoken attitudes, and whatever views you may come to later, you realise those early attitudes are buried pretty deep! We would be trained for some job, to fill in the time till we got married, or just in case we didn't make it and had to be self-supporting.

I think my mother was quite an advanced person for her time, and liked to keep up with the latest theories on child upbringing which she would get from books and magazines. We were allowed to run round naked, and when there was a new baby coming we were allowed to feel it moving, which was a far remove from the gooseberry bush and stork stories of the time. I think a lot of women of her generation were very frustrated because there was little outlet for able women except that of wife and mother. She painted, did photography, played the piano, but unlike her brothers she had never trained for any career.

She died of cancer when I was 13 so I had no mother-daughter relationship during my adolescence. It did make us four girls very dependent on each other, and also independent, as in many ways we were able to make our own decisions. Though we live in different places and lead different lives, we have remained close and always enjoy each other's company.

We were lucky in having lots of books around the house. We were encouraged to read and find out for ourselves and I suppose we were also encouraged to see that one way of coping with the world was to find out how it worked, to know as much about it as possible – perhaps more a head than a heart way of coping. Education was seen as important. It was accepted that I would go to university after

I left secondary school, and do a maths degree – maths was my best subject and I had had an encouraging maths teacher – but I wasn't sure what this would lead to. Teaching was always the main option, but I was not made to be a teacher. I got a scholarship, just scraped in, and that helped.

Though the university was still very small – about 1,000 students altogether – I found it an exciting place. Suddenly the world was a wider place and full of ideas and new people. I found maths was geared to engineering students, not quite my thing, so I changed to psychology (though it was called philosophy then), and it included units in philosophy, logic and ethics. I decided I would rather find out more about how people worked than how numbers did. I eventually got an MA in philosophy.

When I first went to university I lived in a hostel, which was a fairly usual thing for out-of-town students. I hated it. I'd been to boarding school so I'd had enough of that kind of living. It was very strict and the woman who ran it liked to keep an eye on us. She worked on the home-away-from-home principle, which was what I wanted to get away from. Every time we went out she expected us to tell her where we'd been, who we'd gone out with and so on.

My older sister was also working in the city at that time, living with our grandmother, and she'd also had enough of that. So we got our own flat, with another friend who also wanted to leave the hostel, and that was fairly unusual in those days. Members of the family would say things like, 'Are you sure you will feed yourselves properly?' when what they really meant was, 'Are you going to get involved with boys?' Nobody would have dared to say the word pregnant. However, we lived very restrained lives, and over the years had several flats. I suppose, if anything, it taught us responsibility for ourselves.

When I finished my degree, I looked round for a job. The main employers then were the teaching profession and the public service. Not really wanting the former (and I didn't have real teaching subjects), I tried to get into something like Vocational Guidance, which was operating in a limited way, but nothing much doing there. There were so few jobs for other girls at that time. I also had a Diploma in Journalism – a rather theoretical qualification – but there was little for women besides the women's pages. And always in the back of my mind, like so many others, was that what I really wanted to be was a 'writer'.

In the end I got a job in Wellington doing historical research. The attraction of Wellington was that my friend had got a job up there. I lived in a little room in Clifton Terrace where about six of us shared the kitchen and bathroom; my friend flatted with another friend of his on the Terrace. So, as the story goes, in due course we got married and moved to a flat in Kelburn, which seemed like the outer edge of the world. After a while I left work and before too long had two children.

If you had children it was the accepted thing to be at home with them, though at that time, and during the war, more and more women were going into the workforce, those without children being manpowered. Later, with the baby boom, there were more and more women at home. It is easy to forget what a heated issue childcare was then. Kindergartens had been going for some time, but were by no means available everywhere, and playcentres were being set up. Both these looked after older pre-school children for certain times during the week, but if a woman wanted childcare so she could go to work – and there were some of these women around – then they came up against the great current theory of the essential bonding of the first five years.

By that time we had moved to a house in the suburbs and I eventually had five children, four girls and a boy. I don't think we suffered from suburban neurosis. Household chores took up more time and there was not the expectation of too many options. How important expectations are! Most of my friends were in the same situation. I enjoyed having time to myself, rather than rushing out to work, time to read and try to do a bit of writing; I had stories and articles published now and again, and even did a part-time job teaching maths. I think I was quite privileged to have that time.

We had plenty of ideas about bringing up children. After all, I had a degree in psychology. We read about it, discussed it, went to lectures; the playcentres saw one of their main jobs as parent education, and mothers had to do rostered duties to see how it worked. Playcentres probably played a very important part in educating parents, though maybe this reached mainly the middle class. We felt we knew the basics, even if these were not so easy to put into practice. I think we also did a lot of things like being on committees, though not necessarily more than the present-day working mums.

The family roles were still pretty clearly defined. We managed to live modestly on one income. My husband liked to think that was his area and that was okay. I had always had my own post office account with a mini amount in it, including the family benefit – a very enlightened policy for the times, that it was paid to the mother – and an occasional few guineas for something in print. The mother did tend to be more involved with the family, with the father going out to work every day being on the outer, and ours did tend to become a fairly female household. For his time I think my husband did quite a lot with his family; he could be useful in the kitchen, even change the occasional nappy. But the set-up encou raged a certain distance. When he came home from work, it was, 'Dad's tired, don't make too much noise.' So within this little realm I suppose the mother tends to become the decision-maker, the linchpin.

As the children got older, I felt I was not very good at making decisions for them. I might say, 'What I would do is so-and-so', but they had to learn to make their own decisions; they were the ones who had to take the consequences. It's sometimes hard to know how to stop them doing what they want, even legally sometimes, after they are 16. It's hard, too, to know how much guidance you give, spoken or unspoken, intended or unintended.

Hilary was the fourth child, third daughter, and she wasn't an easy child. She had terrible eczema from when she was a few weeks old. She had an awful rash all over her face, and her legs would be covered with it. We tried everything that was available then – nothing helped much, some treatments made it worse. Later it turned to asthma, which she has had to contend with ever since. I don't know whether having an extra problem to cope with has been an influence, but she is a very strong and active and decisive person now.

She was a very shy, clinging child. I remember the times I had to stick around at playcentre because she wouldn't stay on her own, when I was dying for the chance to go off and do something on my own. She was also teased by her outgoing next-older sister. Now she will stand up to anyone, in her quiet way. But she turned into a bright, hard-working child, did well at primary school and later went on to Onslow College. Though it was a bit of a trek by bus and train, after lots of discussion it was decided she would go there. It was a fairly new co-ed school where, by all reports, new ideas were being tried out and her next-older sister had her final year there. Later on, in the fifth form, after a bit of hassling, she acquired a motorbike which, allowing for gale days, did make getting to school much quicker.

During the teenage years, I don't think we found it particularly easy to talk. Everybody goes through the secretive adolescent stage and wants some respect for their privacy. Still, you find more subtle ways to find out what is going on, like, I hate to say, finding something to do near at hand when the phone rings, or talking to their friends, perhaps out of both curiosity and concern. Do we all engage in these dubious ploys?

I think it was accepted that they would all go on to tertiary education, preferably university, and they took courses at secondary school that would lead on to this. They also expected there would be suitable job waiting for them. I don't know if we expected them to marry at some point and have children. It's hard to answer that. Maybe the expectations changed between the oldest and youngest children. You would have to ask each one. Perhaps it was more an expectation that they would or should lead lives that were useful, creative, rewarding, challenging – what do we want for our children? Between them they have acquired a variety of degrees, including one doctorate, various other qualifications, wool classing, weaving, photography, teaching, librarianship and so on. Four of them have children.

They all left home to go flatting, mostly in mixed flats, or to go to other centres. It's amazing how quickly changes in sexual behaviour have become accepted. You know, first the pill came in, then the mini-skirt. Was there a connection?

When the youngest went to school it was time for me to do something else more constructive. By that time, too, the women's movement was on its way, with new opportunities and perhaps new pressures. At that time the transitional courses at Victoria University were being set up, first in sociology and economics, where a graduate could go in at Stage III and do BA Honours in two years. Here was the opportunity. My choice was sociology. I was absolutely terrified but was amazed how the younger students accepted the older ones. The 'mature' student was popping up on campus, but not to the same extent that they are now. Also sociology has always attracted people like public servants doing extra study, so there was a good range of people and ages. It was a time for meeting new people, opening new windows.

When I finished my degree I worked for the Society for Research on Women on a funded survey. Here was real work, a real job with real money. After that I worked in the Sociology Department as a tutor and demonstrator for a number of years – nice flexible hours so I still had some time for myself. And a chance too to work with 'mature' students. It was during this time that Hilary and I went on a trip to China together in the heady days of the seventies.

About this time Hilary began living with her boyfriend. It was still a situation you tended to skate over in conversation with some friends, and it was when she was on a trip overseas she found she was pregnant. We were overseas at the same time. I got her letter just as we left Europe for Hong Kong and opened it somewhere over Asia. We wondered how she would cope and could only write offering support. The friends she was with were also extremely supportive.

She came back, had the baby, and soon the relationship had broken up. She had the support of all the family, and with childcare she was able to keep on working. By this time it was not so unusual for women to be bringing up children alone, thanks partly to the DPB, and the child became part of the family.

Later she formed another relationship and had a son. Then, sadly, her partner was diagnosed as having cancer. When two years later it was diagnosed as terminal, they decided to marry. About the same time her daughter was diagnosed as having leukaemia. They got wonderful service from the public hospital; the car almost came to know the road there by itself. Hilary was the strong one and they became involved in cancer support organisations. Her daughter recovered; sadly, her husband didn't. Quite by chance we lived nearby so we have been able to be on hand for minding and so on, and her son and his grandfather have a good relationship. Without the stresses of work, my husband has mellowed somewhat!

Hilary was always the one who saw herself as not marrying or having children, but as being a career woman. She was, I think, the one I could talk to the most easily, and now I suppose we are sharing more of the same perspective. I've never found it easy to talk to the children about my own problems, perhaps because I'm not very good at that anyway, but I know they would rally in a crisis. I don't know if they feel they have the time hanging over them when their parents won't be able to cope – Alzheimer's or whatever waiting in the wings. Of course, we hope that such situations won't arise, that we will have the good sense to make speedy exits.

I think now that if the children had problems they would ask advice but not necessarily take it. There is a fine line for parents between interference and helpfulness and I hope we know where it lies. After all, we all have our own lives to lead. Perhaps with luck we become 'friends' – a friend with a particular interest and concern and a listening ear.

Four out of five now live in Wellington, and perhaps physical proximity has helped to keep the family in contact. They have gone through changing relationships, 'partner' sometimes replacing 'spouse', and one found the Matrimonial Property Act deals very inadequately with the break-up of a de facto relationship. And what a speedy journey the term 'partner' has made into social acceptance!

As for marriage, I can't help seeing it from a sociological point of view. Such institutions exist to serve certain social purposes which, of course, are changing all the time. You only have to think how last century marriages lasted about 20 years or so, and wonder whether the same set-up can cope with our vastly increased lifespan and so many other social changes. And surely such institutions exist for us and not us for them.

And there's another thing a bit of sociology does for you too – sometimes you see yourself as a role player, fitting into all these different roles, in a way distancing yourself from them, seeing them from the outside, perhaps like a kind of game. But maybe you don't have to be a sociologist to do that. I've been involved in the women's movement for a good many years, and of course there are vastly more opportunities now, but I do feel that I have had choices. I don't see my life as centred round my family, or my children. At least I always liked to think I was getting on with my own life, which could be something quite separate.

I know the women's movement has been two steps forward and one step back and I'm currently reading Susan Faludi's book *Backlash* – so many familiar arguments there. But all the same, looking back you can see the changes have been immense. Take just one small example, the number of women you hear on the radio who are spokesperson for this and that. And I think there have been quite subtle changes in our way of thinking.

I know I've got this thing about time, that commodity which is handed out in 24-hour chunks to us all, too precious to waste, and I'm aware that the children were pressured at least to look busy. Now I've been able to give a bit more of this commodity to an old love – reading and writing poetry – and that has meant new and interesting contacts. And Wellington always has so much to offer, things to do, things to see.

As for the family, we exchange views, share books, and I might go to a film or a show or on a peace or protest march with one or other of them. Some things we would agree on and some not, and that's how it should be. Naturally, parents' views do trickle down, being the earliest they are exposed to, and you hope they will to some extent see eye-to-eye with you. But they have to come to those views by their own efforts.

We try to have family gatherings now and again for birthdays or for Christmas. I think they get on reasonably well together and would give support if necessary. But it is not always easy to see what their view is from the other side of that spectrum. It can be disconcerting! Truth has many faces. As for the role of the mother, I see her as a kind of mediator and, I hate to say it, at times as a kind of manipulator.

Hilary

When people like me remember their childhoods, I think they blank out the bad bits and just remember that it was always summer, with lovely evenings and all the neighbourhood kids playing happily together. Or highlights like somebody getting a television and being allowed to go and watch half-an-hour a week of some terrible American sitcom. And holidays. We went on long holidays at Christmas time and they always had to be somewhere different. It seemed like it always took two days to get there – it was usually North Auckland or somewhere like that. We all loaded into the car, the latest child was on the knee in the front seat, and it was always hot sunny weather. Whereas my mother said we always had terrible weather and everybody fought! I don't remember that. As a child, I do remember having lots of kids to play with and lots of space to play in. And a mother who was always there.

I was terrible at nights with my eczema and asthma but I never remember her being grumpy about getting up several times in the night, even though she had the other children. She had unlimited patience, and was always positive and encouraging. She wasn't very affectionate – we're not very affectionate in our family – but she was the one who was always there, whereas Dad had his work. He had his own small publishing business and worked seven days a week, 24 hours a day, it seemed. When he brought his work home he liked to do his proofs on the sitting-room table, so everybody had to be quiet and creep around. That was a bit impractical – maybe they could have worked out some way for him to have a quiet space. They didn't do that until recently, when they turned one of the bedrooms into a study.

Dad was the authoritarian, stern one, the one who cared about table manners and all those things, whereas I never remember seeing my mother angry or cross. You could see she got a little bit frustrated occasionally and bickered with Dad but I never remember her being angry with the children. Even when I was 13 and I put my foot through the front door in a tantrum because she hadn't bought the right size knitting needles, she didn't seem to be angry, with all the rush of going off to casualty and getting stitched up. I remember Dad being absolutely furious. But that might not be her memory at all! The consequences of that tantrum were so bad that I consciously controlled my temper after that.

When I was at secondary school I suppose the relationship became more distant. I don't think I talked to her about anything serious. I just didn't think that she would understand or it was all too difficult when I did talk to her. She came from rural South Canterbury, her father was the local lawyer and she was sent off to boarding school during the Depression. Whereas I was at school in the time of the Vietnam war, with student protests and tour marches. I was at a co-ed school where the Secondary School Students Association was starting up and politics were really important. We were interested in elections and very interested in the war – we wanted to know about the real world.

I think Mum and Dad were interested in politics. They grew up with Massey's photo on the wall. Dad's politics remained conservative but Mum's became more liberal. I remember when I was about nine, the Taiwanese ambassador's child in my class said in school news what a terrible place communist China was and how they killed people all the time. I went home and asked Mum whether that was true, and she had her usual broad-minded approach, saying that people have different interpretations of things and we don't always know what is really happening. Later on, in 1976, we actually went to China together on a New Zealand–China Society tour. I think she was battling with the (Anglican) church as well, because she had a Unitarian stage and refused to have any of us younger ones baptised, in spite of her father-in-law's disapproval.

Mum was always interested in ideas. We were always reading and always had lots of magazines like the *New Statesman* and the New Zealand *Monthly Review*. She got the latest ones from the library – we went down every week to choose our books.

I was very shy and quiet. I didn't go out with boys or anything like that, so that was not much of an issue, but the political thing was. Later, at university, I remember Dad putting his foot down when I said I wanted to go out to some anti-tour march at four o'clock in the morning at the airport, following Tim Shadbolt. He absolutely refused, saying he wasn't going to let me do that. I suppose I was about 19 and still at home.

I went to university when I was 16. Nobody wanted to go to the seventh form then – you left school to do something much more exciting as soon as you could. At university you didn't have to work too hard until the last few weeks, so you could spend your time socialising in the cafe or going to concerts and just cram for finals. It didn't matter. Nowadays people have stopped treating university as an interesting, stimulating place. It's somewhere where you have to sit down and work, and students have stopped protesting about anything except money.

I didn't leave home until I left university and went to Library School – I was still only about 20 then. It was cheaper to live at home. While at university, I worked 10 hours a week at the university library for $1 an hour, so that was $10 a week which was enough to pay for luxuries, plus I had a bursary of about $200 a year, which was a huge amount. And we were paid to go to Library School then, about $3,000 a year, which seemed a fortune.

Mum had gone back to university by then, got another degree and started working, so she was into a whole new thing. She was doing a paid job for the first time since she married, working on the Employers' Attitudes Survey, so all through my later adolescence she was into her own thing. I don't remember there being much communication between us at that time. I think it's probably quite common – you depend on your mother when you are a child, then she becomes almost irrelevant, and when you have your own children she's suddenly incredibly important again: then you depend on your parents for all sorts of things, if your relationship is good.

After Library School, I worked in libraries for a few years. I had left home and was living with a guy in a flat. When that relationship ended I went overseas, but when I arrived in London I discovered I was pregnant. It was a difficult decision to go ahead with the pregnancy but I took a chance on my parents and friends being supportive, and they were.

Mum and Dad were travelling overseas at the same time and I didn't know what to tell Mum. I didn't know what to do about anything really, but they were great. I came back when I was about five months pregnant – they were back by then and I got bits and pieces of work until my daughter was born a few months later. Dad was in the process of winding his business down a bit so I did some work with him, along with little bits of library work. They were very supportive. The family had a history of unusual relationships, so they'd got used to not having any conventionally married children doing the regular thing.

I lived with my daughter's father briefly, but it was a pretty disastrous situation all round. We had no money and I had to take jobs wherever I could before and after she was born. My parents helped me in lots of practical ways, babysitting, lending us their car and buying us a drier.

A little after that I met Max and we eventually moved in together and had a regular lifestyle in a nuclear family. We lived quite near my parents, which was a total coincidence. Max had decided he wanted to buy a house so he started looking around in other places, then the real estate agent said, 'I've got another one in your price range', so we came to look at this one. It was in two flats and I thought, quite negatively, that it was just like my parents' house – same outlook, same style, and only half a mile away. However, it turned out to be very fortuitous.

Max had a good job which he enjoyed, and a good income, I became pregnant and we were set to be a normal middle-class family. Then he got cancer and after a couple of years it was obvious that it was terminal. He lived for four years after it was diagnosed. It's a time when you live from day to day, so you don't actually analyse it as you go through. Mum was totally supportive again. In fact, when Max was having treatment, my daughter had leukaemia as well, so there was lots of childcare to do. Mum and Dad were always there, stepping in to look after my young son. When Max finally realised his cancer was terminal, we decided to get married and have a big party – we did that and it was a good thing to do socially and legally.

Mum leads a very busy life, she fills it up with all sorts of things, but she always seems to have time for us. Her outlook is always so positive. If she has the children she'll always say they're perfectly well-behaved. My father's the opposite – he says they grizzled or moaned or something. Totally different perceptions of the same thing!

Our lives and our expectations have been quite different. There's about 38 years between us in age, so our experiences have been quite different too. She came from a professional middle-class upbringing where everybody's social status was sorted out. I guess when she had children, she thought we would all have regular nuclear family lives, but none of us really did, nobody really fitted into that mould. Only one out of the five of us is currently married and living as a nuclear family.

But it was always clear that education was really important so we succeeded with that. It was expected that we all got not only degrees, but post-graduate qualifications as well. There was never any question of our going to university: it was just there and everybody went. I suppose it was free then, or cheaper, and there were always holiday jobs around or jobs to keep you going. There was always the thought that I'd have a career, or something like a career, and earn my own living – I was never ever going to be dependent on anybody else for an income – and I have really done that, with a bit of help from the state here and there.

Mum's life was very centred in the home. She and Dad had a car which wouldn't have been accessible to a lot of people at that time, but things were delivered then – you rang up and the groceries were delivered, the bread was delivered. You went to the fruit shop and the library on Saturday mornings. The house and the children were Mum's domain and I don't think she even wanted Dad around. Every time she went off to have another baby she said, 'Goodbye, see you in two weeks' time', sort of thing. She wouldn't want him anywhere near her, fussing around. There's the expectation of much more shared parenting now. And I guess her community would have been more local, although I don't know whether that actually happened in reality. Now you can live in a street but never see your neighbours, and have all your social life with your work or your friends who may be miles away.

Mum didn't ever talk about women's roles – she just did it and she didn't ever put limits on what we could do. She always did all the wallpapering and retiling the floors and things like that. She did all the cooking and the child-minding, and she seemed to make all the decisions, although I guess she didn't. And she still doesn't have anything to do with the finances. That's Dad's role. He hands over the housekeeping, whereas I've always known exactly what comes in and out of the house, and what you need. Even if things were difficult in Dad's business, and they were from time to time, nobody knew about it. It was never obvious in the rest of the household. Whether even she knew I don't know – he was just grumpy and worked longer hours – but it was never something that anybody else could have an input into.

But there was one thing that was different about her from other mothers – she was always so intellectual, ideas were important. And she does things fast, doesn't waste time on things. She walks fast, she talks fast – there wasn't always a lot of time for things like affection. Her and Dad's idea of a holiday was not to go for a little while then stop at a nice restaurant and enjoy it in a leisurely way. Nothing was leisurely – it was always done with a purpose. They love travelling overseas but it's three days per country, that's enough: let's not go back there, let's go somewhere different now. No time to sit back and enjoy it. I like to be able to put my feet up, but I can't do that. I feel bad about staying in bed in the morning and reading. Mum would say that she does spend time on herself but her idea of spending time on herself is running the Poetry Society or reading a magazine. She reads so fast – she can flick through it and say, 'I've read that now.'

I have inherited a great sense of duty from her – that you have to look after other people all the time and your needs aren't terribly important. It's your duty to take an interest in other people's ideas and other people. I've been trying to do a little project on the history of our local playcentre and I've been looking at the old minutes when Mum was involved. In there it says So-and-so did this, So-and-so organised coffee-morning flowers, and Mum suggested that we set up local WEA [Workers Education Association] courses! There's always that self-improvement aspect. So I've always got involved in community things, which she did too. When I'm involved in organisations I have trouble getting out of them, I find it hard to say no to anybody. I don't really resent that, but it is a common issue for women. It just amazes me that men say, 'Oh, that's their problem, don't worry about it', and here I am having agonies about how I have offended somebody or what I've done wrong and how I can improve it. Max was good like that, because he didn't dwell on things as his responsibility when there was nothing more he could do about them. Part of me likes that community involvement and at the moment I would love to stand for the Board of Trustees of my son's school, but as a single parent it's very difficult.

I don't see Mum so much now just to have talks with her about the meaning of life. It's more practical things, like, 'Here are the children, I'm going off to aerobics'. I like to do things for myself, and will go out of my way to get to my aerobic dance class or my walking group. I take the children out through howling southerlies to get dropped at my parents' place so I can go. I need to do those few things.

My daughter's life will be different again. She's grown up in a single-parent family. She has got a father, he's around but he's not that supportive. And I guess that we are much less well off financially and she's much more socially aware than I was as a small child. The children know where everybody fits in the socio-economic field these days, so she knows exactly where she is in relation to the rest of the children in her class. Tertiary education will be a huge expense for us if she chooses to go.

I hope as she gets older that she won't feel that I'm too remote or not interested or wouldn't understand. Especially from adolescence on. She's the oldest, and I think it's difficult for the oldest, so I hope to be more responsive and there more for her. On the other hand, I might just get too busy and not be available. I'll have to watch it. I'm really pleased that I have children but sometimes it's such hard work, especially being a single parent and having to be so careful with money.

One of her big things now is that I go out too much. I don't go out much at all, but it's too much for her. I try to keep it down to one meeting or outing a week, but she still complains about me going to my aerobic dance classes or working in the school holidays because I should be at home – real mothers are. She has this idea that real mothers are there at home for everyone, cooking and cleaning. She was surprised when I went through her peers' parents and found out how few actually fitted this mould. Most of my friends have paid work or are looking for it. Even women who have maybe two or three children either expect that they will go back to something eventually or still see themselves as having a career. A lot just take a year's maternity leave, then go back for 20 hours a week – and childcare is now such an important issue. So it's very rare for somebody to actually give up and not go back for, say, 10 years, whereas in Mum's generation women stopped work when they got married. The expectations were so different then.

The world's changed so much since Mum was young but she has changed with it. I'm sure she wouldn't – and neither would I – look back to some golden age, when everything was so much better, which it really wasn't. Just from the practical point of view, if my daughter had got leukaemia 30 years ago she would never have survived. Suburban neurosis was a real thing then for many women, and so was domestic violence, even though it wasn't talked about. So she has changed with the times. She reads such a lot too. It's much harder for Dad, being a more negative person, although he has changed over the years too and become much more liberal. We have all inherited bits from her but unfortunately not the whole package, like her looks. I like to have Mum as a role model – I'd like to have such an interest in people and always see their good points like she does. She's in her seventies now, so she won't be round for ever. I don't know what I'd do without her.

Conclusion

From this journey through other women's lives, many images come to mind. Some have to do with the changing social, economic and legal context of women's lives, others are of the specific experiences of individual mothers and daughters.

The major national and international events of the last 75 years inevitably surface in these women's lives – the First World War, the influenza epidemic, the Depression, the Second World War, the Korean War and the Vietnam War. But it is often smaller events that shape the social framework for women – for example, the opening of the first birth control clinic in 1953 (ironically around the same time as the Mazengarb Report on 'promiscuous' behaviour among teenagers), the development of kindergartens and playcentres, the introduction of six o'clock (and later 10 o'clock) closing in hotels, the passing of the Government Service Equal Pay Act in 1960 and the Matrimonial Property Act in 1976, the United Women's Conventions in the seventies, the Hite Report of 1976 and the introduction of the Domestic Purposes Benefit in 1973.

Perhaps the most dramatic change in women's lives recorded in this book has been the nature of women's work. Women have always worked, but over the three generations described the emphasis has shifted from physical home-centred work, to child and family-centred work and then to paid work outside the home. However, instead of replacing one style of work with another, each generation has simply added its own new focus to the one before. As Joanne commented rather ruefully, 'In a way it was simpler in those days, because your choices were really limited – you either pursued your career or got married and had kids. Now we try to do both . . . I am finding the balancing act very difficult.'

Almost without exception the mothers described their mothers as hard-working and stoic. While some of the older women were frustrated by an inability to use their talents for anything other than recreation – only a few were able to use their skills to supplement the family income – others were so preoccupied with keeping their households running that they had little time or energy for affection or fun.

The next generation had more labour-saving devices, but still felt they had to fill every minute of the day. Anne commented, 'I never ever saw my mother idle. It was quite sad in a way, because if she ever did take a break, it was almost a guilty thing for her.' The mothers were parenting during the post-war period when the push for women to return to the home was at its height.[1] They made a career of being wives and mothers and when they took on paid work it was usually from necessity rather than choice. But this busy devotion to housekeeping and childrearing irritated many daughters, who felt that their mothers could have made different and better use of their time. In fact, several were so sure that their mothers had underused their talents and given away too much of themselves, that they made a conscious decision to be different: 'I don't want my life to be like my Mum's. I don't actually want to be available to everybody'; 'I don't want to be a doormat.'

The daughters' frustration at their mothers' lives was somewhat ironic, given that most of them looked back on their childhoods as a happy and even idyllic time, partly because their mother was always there for them. Perhaps it is a luxury of adulthood to be able to criticise our mothers' lifestyle having thoroughly enjoyed its benefits.

Some mothers consciously or unconsciously enabled their daughters to make different choices by encouraging them to do well at school. In the 1930s, when most of the mothers were growing up, the country was in the grip of an economic depression. One effect of this was to limit the mothers' educational opportunities. Alison wanted to be a Karitane nurse, but 'you had to pay for your training and Mum and Dad couldn't afford it'. She was determined her daughter would have a better opportunity. Lynda now has a university degree, along with other qualifications. Alice left school at 12 because 'Mum couldn't afford to buy school uniforms'. Her daughter also has a university degree and several certificates and diplomas. In fact, 10 of the 14 daughters have higher qualifications than their mothers, and they, along with the four who achieved at much the same level, have been much more likely to use their qualifications in paid work. Joanne is a lawyer, Frances a qualified accountant, Hilary a librarian, Marian a psychologist and Ruth manages a business. None of these jobs can be done from home and none combines particularly easily with caring for young children. Some mothers did not foresee the extent to which daughters would seek to combine work with childcare, or that some would decide not to have children.

Childcare has been a constant worry for mothers who have had to work to survive, or who have chosen to use their talents in paid work while bringing up their children. There have been some improvements over the last 30 years, but not enough. Gwitha had to take live-in jobs so she could keep her daughter with her; Alice at first shared childcare with her husband while she ran her hairdressing business then worked from home. Daughters experienced similar problems. Childcare was a nightmare for both Hilary and Jane, who relied heavily on their mothers for support.

One way for women to reduce the pressures of combining childcare and a career is to have fewer children. This can either reduce the time women are out of the workforce or make arranging childcare marginally less complicated. It is probably no coincidence that all but one of the daughters had fewer children than her mother and three have had no children at all.

While women have taken advantage of reliable contraception and satisfying alternatives to increase their options, their lives have also been made easier by changes in the law and limited government recognition of the work women do in bringing up children.

The Matrimonial Property Act was passed in 1976. It played an important part in enabling women to leave violent or abusive marriages. Two of the mothers in this book would have left their husbands earlier had they been able to be financially independent. Such a move would have improved their children's lives as well as their own. Peggy was one of these, and vividly remembered the difficulties facing women who wished to leave a marriage: 'I couldn't leave – there was nowhere to go, no money and if you left, you left with what you stood up in. You couldn't take a thing from the family home. You were just a chattel compared to now.'

Perhaps even more significant than the Matrimonial Property Act was the introduction of the Domestic Purposes Benefit (DPB) in 1973. No fewer than nine of the 26 women in this book either did benefit or would have benefited from this support. The DPB enabled Hilary to support her daughter and Lowana to keep her son. It would have transformed Gwitha's life and taken pressure off Jean and Peggy – 'Having some government support, you don't have to stay because you've got no other choice. There was nowhere for Mum to go.'

The changes I have described, whether legal, technological or economic, have altered the landscape in which women live. This means each generation has had to adapt to a different social environment while at the same time maintaining a personal link with the generations on either side. How do women manage this task? With difficulty sometimes, but more often with flexibility, openness and trust, and a willingess, especially on the mothers' part, to keep the door to communication open. When daughters got into difficult or unexpected situations, as with Joanne's live-in relationship, Lowana's pregnancy and Jane's early marriage, the importance of keeping the link going generally outweighed any desire to criticise or judge. Good will – and the relationship – prevailed.

Relationships between individual mothers and daughters tend to follow a natural pattern. Daughters begin their lives totally dependent on their mothers. As they grow older, they move steadily towards independence, with the pace accelerating during adolescence. Most daughters spend their early adulthood experimenting with different lifestyles and exploring a range of experiences, not all of which they are willing to share with their mothers. Eventually many of them marry or settle into a relationship and have children themselves, which brings them closer to their mothers' experience and hence to a more equal relationship.

Mothers do not stay still either. As their children become less dependent, they are more free to expand their own lives outside the family. They may return to work or study, develop new leisure interests, set up a business or leave an unhappy marriage. Their choices are as wide as their daughters', and many women enjoy their new-found freedom.[2] However, very few move so far that they jeopardise their relationships with their families, particularly their daughters.

Grandchildren are an important link between mother and daughter. Sometimes for the first time, the daughters in this book understood their mothers' lives and the choices they had made. In turn, mothers had expertise and confidence in an area where their daughters did not. They could and usually did provide practical and emotional support. Wherever this aspect of the relationship broke down or was unsatisfying, there was a sense that an important strand in the link between mother and daughter was missing.

While most mother-daughter relationships follow the pattern of closeness, moving apart and a return to closeness, the actual timing of moves can vary depending on circumstances. For example, not all daughters have children, and in this situation mother and daughter have to find another connection, usually through shared interests rather than work. Indeed, some mothers in the book felt left behind by their daughters' work achievements, which increased rather than reduced the gap between them.

Sometimes mothers act in ways that surprise or frustrate their daughters. Marie is not the grandmother Joanne expected her to be, and because Lisa came to motherhood without a 'working model' she had to learn her mothering skills 'on the job'. Three mothers married men whose violent behaviour or alcoholism intervened in the mother-daughter relationship and another put her religious principles ahead of her relationship with her lesbian daughter.

Whenever the pattern differed from the norm, mothers and daughters had to work hard to keep their relationship strong. Most have been successful, with tolerance, trust and acceptance on both sides the key to success.

In a number of stories in this book, patterns of behaviour were repeated between generations; in other cases, the patterns were consciously changed. Changes were particularly apparent in styles of communication. The first generation of women described in this book – the mothers' mothers – were excellent providers, but only a few could be described as models of openness and flexibility. Their daughters remembered their stoicism and reticence, rather than their warmth: 'She never said anything, she made the best of it to us kids'; 'Hide it all and have a good clean happy home, that was the way'; 'I don't remember her being very emotional, not too many hugs and kisses.'

Fortunately, growing up in such an environment was enough to encourage some of the daughters to do things differently, to be more open, more informative, more tolerant and more trusting. Their daughters appreciated this and have continued the trend, with generally positive results. This is just as well, because whether they like it or not, the relationship between mothers and daughters is for life. In one form or another, it persists through childhood, adolescence, marriage, having children, going out to work and old age, and is broken only when one of the partners dies. Even then, its impact may remain.

Most of the relationships in this book have survived and survived well. Mothers and daughters enjoy each other's company and accept the differences between them. They share ideas, coffee, books, shopping trips, affection, practical support and laughs. They were a pleasure to be with, together and separately. Some mothers and daughters are not so close but they talked with honesty and concern all the same, regretting the distance between them. I appreciated that.

For myself, a lot has changed between the beginning and ending of this book. I am still sorry that Mum didn't let me go earlier, sending me into the world with her blessing and support rather than with fear and suspicion. That didn't happen and I survived. More importantly, we survived. I have learned in the course of compiling this book that while tolerance, acceptance and forgiveness are great qualities for mothers of any age, they are also useful attributes for daughters. I have come to appreciate my mother's strengths and the difficulties she had to cope with. I realise that she was not alone in her struggles. I value even more the time we have together – my heart skips a beat when the phone rings in the night, in case she is in trouble.

I have also come to value my own daughters who are fine examples of the younger generation, being more tolerant, forgiving and accepting in their twenties than I was in my thirties and beyond. The thread that links the generations is in good hands.

1 See, for example, Helen May, *Minding Children, Managing Men: Conflict and Compromise in the Lives of Postwar Pakeha Women*, Bridget Williams Books, Wellington, 1992.

2 See, for example, Alison Gray, *Springs in My Heels*, Bridget Williams Books, Wellington, 1991.

and accepting in their twenties than I was in my thirties and beyond. The thread that links the generations is in good hands.

1 See, for example, Helen May, *Minding Children, Managing Men: Conflict and Compromise in the Lives of Postwar Pakeha Women*, Bridget Williams Books, Wellington, 1992.

2 See, for example, Alison Gray, *Springs in My Heels*, Bridget Williams Books, Wellington, [illegible].